Teamwork:

Involving People in Quality and Productivity Improvement

dedicated to our parents

Chuck and Ruth Aubrey
and
John and Mildred Felkins

G A 8 8 0 0 8 9 2

Teamwork:

Involving People in Quality and Productivity Improvement
Charles A. Aubrey, II
and
Patricia K. Felkins

QUALITY PRESS
American Society for Quality Control
Milwaukee, Wisconsin

UNIPUB/QUALITY RESOURCES
A Division of Kraus-Thomson Organization Limited
White Plains, New York

First Printing 1988
Second Printing 1988
Third Printing 1989

Printed in the United States of America

UNIPUB/Quality Resources
A Division of Kraus-Thomson Organization Limited,
One Water Street, White Plains, New York 10601

Library of Congress Cataloging-in-Publication Data

Aubrey, Charles A.
  Teamwork.

  Includes bibliographies and index.
  1. Management—Employee participation.   2. Quality
circles.   I. Felkins, Patricia K.   II. Title.
HD5650.A84   1988   658.3′152   87–37927
ISBN 0-527-91626-9 (Unipub/Quality Resources)

CONTENTS

CONTENTS

INTRODUCTION
Teamwork: Employee Involvement in Quality and Productivity Improvement

Today management must be more creative and innovative in meeting the challenges of declining productivity, increasing foreign competition, and a work force that may not be motivated by traditional management practices.

At one time the majority of American workers were in manufacturing rather than service. Now the number of service jobs exceeds those in the manufacturing area. The productivity and quality of the service economy are essential to America's sustained economic growth and standard of living.

Employee involvement is one approach to improving quality and productivity with cooperative relationships, open communication, and group problem solving and decision making. This approach received substantial credit for contributing to quality and productivity improvement in a number of countries, especially in Japan. Participation and employee involvement have also been successful in the United States in both manufacturing and service industries.

The participative process may be characterized by several types of employee groups. Some of the most common terms are *quality circles, quality improvement teams, productivity teams,* and *employee involvement groups.* There are also *idea groups, winners' circles,* and *progress groups* that reflect specific needs and organizational cultures. In this book, *team* or *group* will refer to a variety of employee involvement contexts.

In all cases, these are groups of employees who volunteer to be trained in problem-solving techniques and who have the improvement of quality and productivity within the organization as their primary goal.

It is estimated that there are now approximately two hundred thousand employee involvement groups in the United States and several million operating worldwide. Participation and employee involvement are relatively new techniques in the United States, bringing substantial opportunities for improvement and innovation by effectively increasing productivity and quality as well as providing greater cost reduction and improved work satisfaction. This is accomplished through the projects the quality teams complete, and through the integration of the philosophy into each person's day-to-day job, thus helping to increase overall quality and productivity in a highly competitive marketplace.

CHAPTER 1
Participation and Employee Involvement

Participation is a process that grows out of individual and organizational needs. People participate in community, social, and political groups. The motivation to be involved in meaningful work may be used to increase commitment, productivity, and innovation in the organization. When individual and organizational goals are integrated successfully, the results support business and personal growth. This creates the best possible team approach for improving quality and productivity.

Basic Principles of Participation

Participative philosophy is based on the belief that employees will take more pride and interest if they are allowed to make meaningful contributions to their work and influence decisions made about it. Active employee participation and involvement in the decision-making process can increase commitment and accomplishment. Employees are able to express their work-related concerns, improve their jobs, and contribute to the fulfillment of organizational goals and objectives. A crucial premise is that the individual who is doing the job is the expert and knows best how the process could be improved. By allowing employee input into decisions regarding their work, management acknowledges that these people are a vast resource of knowledge and ideas. Involvement groups are meant to bring human abilities into full play and reveal the potential of the work force. In this sense, team implementation symbolizes the company's endorsement of the creativity and ''brainpower'' waiting to be expressed within the work force.

Participation and employee involvement evolved through a merging of behavioral and management science with quality control sciences. Chris Argyris[1] and Rensis Likert[2] helped to identify the need for cooperation between employees and management in reaching organizational goals and improving operations. Likert lists three primary characteristics of the most effective form of management which he calls *System 4:* (1) supportive relationships, (2) group decision making and group methods, and (3) high performance goals. There are also other key figures in the theoretical base of participation including Douglas McGregor, Frederick Herzberg, and A. H. Maslow.

McGregor's *Theory Y* is the underlying attitude required for employee involvement. McGregor attached the *Y* label to managerial assumptions that recognize the intellectual and creative potential of the average human being. Quality teams use this potential by involving people at all employee levels in solving quality or other work-related problems. By giving employees training, time for meetings, and recognition, the corporation shows that it believes employees have meaningful contributions to make. The opposite assumption, which McGregor calls *Theory X,* is that employees are lazy, do not like work, and do not want to take responsibility.[3]

William G. Ouchi's more recent *Theory Z* builds on the best of these assumptions in relation to Japanese business success. According to Ouchi, egalitarianism is a central feature of Z organizations. It is assumed that employees can apply discretion and work autonomously without close supervision because they are trusted. Z organizations are characterized by commitment and loyalty to the organization.[4]

Herzberg's motivation theory is another management philosophy that is a foundation for participation and employee involvement. In developing and promoting this theory, Herzberg stresses that growth and individual development are derived from the content of the job itself. Factors that contribute to the fulfillment of a job are the opportunity for new learning, direct communication between management and employees, regular feedback, and personal accountability. Achievement, recognition, and responsibility are primary motivators for people at work. Herzberg also examines "hygiene factors," such as working conditions, policy, and relationships that can make an individual dissatisfied with a job, but do not necessarily motivate that individual.[5]

Maslow's hierarchy of needs is often cited in relation to motivation within the participative process. The hierarchy begins with basic needs and moves through a sequence of increasingly higher level needs from security and safety, to social needs, to esteem needs, and then to the highest level need, *self-actualization.* When employees channel their energies at work to achieve higher needs, they show increased interest and motivation toward work.[6] Participation and employee involvement provide people with a vehicle for attaining personal goals and fulfilling their motivational needs. Transforming these behavioral science concepts into operational guidelines (Table 1.1) enables the participative philosophy to be both theoretically sound and functionally applicable.

Actual team practice relates to this basic philosophy. If participation is to be successful, critical elements must be maintained and followed. The following is a list of some of these elements:

- The teams implemented must have the development of the team members' individual capabilities as one of their objectives. If teams are used by management solely as a cost-reduction program, or to manipulate employees for the organization's benefit, the program will fail.

- Management at all levels must support team efforts openly and unreservedly. Managers and supervisors should not feel threatened, or take credit away from the team when improvements are made. Involvement in team activities can enhance trust and cooperation between managers and team members. However, managers may believe that they are in a vulnerable position because

TABLE 1.1

Behavioral Science Concept	Employee Involvement Application
Management must be committed to change and involved in its initiation.	An employee team effort is initiated only on the decision of senior management. Members work with their supervisors to choose priority problems.
People should have control in deciding or changing work elements in their areas.	Teams are made up of workers with a common area of interest and intervention. Changes are related to the work each person does daily.
Individuals should not be coerced to change.	Participation in teams is voluntary for nonmanagement personnel.
Work should be intrinsically motivating and enriching.	Team members learn new skills in problem solving, statistics, and measurement. They are given responsibility for improving their work area.
Change efforts should be measured for impact.	All team activities are monitored and evaluated on a regular basis. Teams also assess their own performance and results.
Jobs need feedback to be reinforcing.	Members receive regular feedback from their supervisor. Management also provides comments after the team presentation.
People need opportunities to meet higher motivational needs through their jobs.	The intrinsic value of bringing change and improvement, and the direct interaction with management provides recognition and support of individual and team development.

of current trends to decrease management levels and numbers. In a recent personnel survey half of all respondents indicated that managers in their organizations had trouble coping with employees who wanted more autonomy and mobility.[7] Yet, the support and involvement of management is crucial to the success of any program. Lack of management support is the number one cause of failure.

■ Membership in teams should be voluntary. If employees are forced to participate, they may believe that the process is just a facade or a management gimmick to make people work harder.

■ Team spirit and group effort must be developed. Projects are not individual efforts. Team members should solve problems together and help each other learn and develop new skills. No criticism of people is allowed at any point in the process. The team must focus on the problem, not on personalities.

All recognition should be centered on the group rather than on specific individuals.

■ Creativity and innovation should be encouraged. A nonthreatening, open atmosphere can be established and maintained in group meetings and management presentations. The leader must ensure that no members dominate the discussions, or, conversely, feel limited in what they can express and contribute.

■ The projects selected by the team members should relate directly to their work. The steering or advisory committee sets the general goals, objectives, and policies, and the teams choose the focus and procedures to meet these goals. Members become more responsible for their work when involved in making decisions regarding that work.

■ Practical training in problem-solving techniques must be provided and used. It is essential that team members have the tools and skills needed to find solutions and make recommendations on the projects they select.

■ An important goal stated by Kaoru Ishikawa is the emphasis on quality awareness and improvement among the work force.[8] Developing a problem-solving capability in employees and fostering an attitude of problem prevention must prevail throughout all team activities. Working on quality issues is the disciplining structure for group involvement and interaction. Not only does this structure prevent the meetings from becoming "gripe" sessions, but many times the solutions recommended by the teams result in substantial cost savings and productivity improvements. In addition to increased feelings of accomplishment and satisfaction among the team members, active employee participation and involvement promote and enhance quality and productivity, reduce costs, and ultimately contribute to the fulfillment of personal and organizational goals and objectives.

Historical Perspectives

Historically, involvement teams have had a common identity and goal. The following is a characteristic definition: small groups of people who do similar work, voluntarily meet on a regular basis to identify and analyze causes of problems, recommend their solutions to management, and, where possible, implement the solutions.

It is important to understand that these teams or groups are not programs with a designated end, nor a cure-all for every quality or productivity problem. Ideally, the teams are part of a continuous process of improvement and development. This process can supplement current managerial practices and benefit the entire organization.

Employee involvement is also a commitment to a particular management style intended to maximize people resources through discovering and using the creative and innovative power within the work force. With proper presentation, education, and conformance to basic principles, these teams can be an integral part of the quality management process by ensuring high quality services and contributing to greater satisfaction and integration among the work force. The success of this process is most evident in Japan.

Quality circles originated in Japan in the early 1960s as part of a drive for quality and a critical economic need to overcome a reputation for cheap, poorly made goods. W. Edwards Deming[9] and J. M. Juran[10] introduced the concepts of statistical quality control and quality management to the Japanese. Dr. Ishikawa, merging these two disciplines, created a system called *quality control circles*. In 1961, a series of exploratory meetings were sponsored by the Union of Japanese Scientists and Engineers (JUSE) under the leadership of Dr. Ishikawa, an engineering professor at the University of Tokyo. The objective was to develop a way for hands-on workers to contribute to the company. In 1962, the first circle was registered with JUSE, and a total of twenty circles were registered and operating by the end of the year. Since that time, quality circle techniques have been taught to and applied by the entire Japanese work force. Today, there are an estimated one million quality circles in Japan with over ten million members. These groups are considered a major contributor to Japan's present status as a leader in both quality and productivity.

Quality circles were first introduced in the United States in 1970 by Lockheed Aircraft, a large manufacturing company. The success of the Lockheed program, combined with the company's enthusiasm in publicizing and promoting its implementation process and results, encouraged other American companies to adopt the participative process. Initially these quality groups were almost exclusively limited to manufacturing industries, but recently, teams have been introduced successfully into service industries.

People and Participation

The Proud Producers, Wizards of Wisdom, Problem Zappers, Finishing Touch, the Innovators, Circle of Iron, Trouble Shooters, Sweet Success, and Counter Intelligents are some of the names employees have given their quality circles, involvement groups, and improvement teams. Each of these names has a special significance for the group. For example, the letters in a team named VOICES represent Visibility, Organization, Integrity, Communication, Efficiency, and Simplicity. There are countless other titles—Jeff's Jets, Hauling Truckers, Denim Blue Devils, Quality Pacers, the Perfect Circle, the Pathfinders—that give some clues as to what is happening with these employee groups in the workplace. Participative teams such as these focus on improved quality and productivity, but people and organizational relationships are being changed in the process. The group names reflect pride in work and awareness of quality as well as commitment and responsibility. These people feel good about themselves and their contribution to the organization.

"Members seem to view their jobs as more important, and their interaction with co-workers has improved," remarked a quality team leader. "This is my hour," a woman explained as she described her experiences as an employee involvement group member. Another person said, "It makes you feel important." Group members are always ready to talk about their team accomplishments, "Our departmental productivity increased. It was one hundred percent better than last year." While these statements clearly reflect positive individual motivation, they also signal a belief that participative groups can make a difference within an organization.

The sense of pride is also evident in this article written for a quality circle newsletter. The writer is a member describing her participative team:

> We are the SECRETARIATS—not to be confused with the great racing champion even though we often "race" to beat the clock. We are eight secretaries who work in different areas and have diverse interests. Our members include a shutterbug, a crafty devil, a frustrated diva, Ms. Nimble Fingers, a jigsaw puzzle expert, a racqueteer, an apprentice seamstress, and a young woman who is always busy with new projects.
>
> We meet each Tuesday as a quality circle because we have one big interest in common—the triple crown of INVOLVEMENT: (1) we want to become more involved in the day-to-day operations of the various administrative divisions to which we are assigned, (2) we want to make our jobs more challenging, and (3) we want to become an integral part of our organizational team effort.

The participative process that works best involves people in reaching business goals. Employee teams learn more about how the organization functions and how they can make their area work better. These groups are not "feel better," interpersonal encounters or expensive suggestion programs. As James E. Olson, president of AT&T, stated, "People want to be part of a quality company. And that means you get your people—every last worker—to realize that what they do is important."[11] Every employee in the organization plays a part in the overall quality of service. This means that employees need both information and opportunities for involvement.

Participative groups such as quality circles initially were created to meet specific business needs in the areas of quality control and production efficiency. Industrial engineers were working on a statistical model, not the people perspective shared by social scientists and psychologists. Participative groups do make a direct contribution to bottom line business success. The skills that employees learn help the organization meet competitive challenges and use resources more effectively. The fact that people are also developed in the process is an important advantage.

Most Fortune 500 companies have some type of participative group or employee involvement. Participation is most often at the basic operating level rather than at the strategic or administrative level. However, in some organizations, interdepartmental management teams and teams including managers, supervisors, and union foremen have been highly successful. The amount of participation and the impact of the process varies greatly. Presently, the most exciting opportunities for participative groups are in service industries such as financial institutions, insurance, health care, and government. These white collar groups are especially significant because they represent the majority of the work force. There are also many possibilities for improving quality, performance, productivity, and customer service.[12]

Today, organizations must have strength in physical and financial resources as well as flexibility in adapting to change. A major part of this change is brought about by new technology. Technological innovation already has affected many work tasks and, in some cases, the overall structure of work and work relationships. More autonomy and participation are evident in the workplace as well as increased interest in the human elements such as team building and motivation. Still, the ultimate organizational goal is economics. The old approach to productivity stressed profit, before quality. Today quality is viewed as a way to maintain long-term profit. Management has realized that individual employees can help to establish and maintain this quality.

Millions of dollars of cost savings and records of increased efficiency and productivity have been attributed to the participative process in manufacturing industries. The participative process of employee involvement and problem solving has hardly begun in the service sector. Yet figures indicate that in some service organizations the return on investment for participation is as high as eight to one after several years of operation. The possibilities for increased productivity and cost savings are great. Customer satisfaction is also a direct result of improved quality and service.

In an effective process, both management and employees share a commitment to quality. A recent event at a small manufacturing firm illustrates the power of unified goals and improved communication between management and employees. A companywide attitude survey revealed that employees had a substantial interest in quality. In fact, some statements from employees indicated that they thought workers had a greater desire for quality than management did. One of the most common concerns expressed by employees was that supervisors pushed people to meet shipping and delivery deadlines at the expense of quality control. The president was amazed at the concern his employees showed for overall quality. To show his commitment, he shut down the organization for an entire day and all the employees met to talk about quality and productivity. One of the most important results of this meeting was the initiation of ongoing employee problem solving groups throughout the organization and greater employee involvement in quality control. Both the president and the employees were motivated to succeed as a team in meeting organizational goals.

Work and Motivation

Defining perceptions and motivations in relation to work helps to clarify the perspective of people toward involvement and participation. Today most employees have more specialized knowledge and skills than many employees had in past years. However, they are not always given more responsibility to match their increased competence. Because of this, many of these people may become alienated or apathetic. Education has also been shown to increase employee needs for greater influence in the workplace.[13]

Employee motivation factors are changing, especially among some of the "gold collar" professionals and technology experts. A study of high technology engineers indicated that traditional reward and recognition systems were not strong motivators. These skilled professionals preferred to work in organizations that practiced participative management in giving employees an opportunity to use their initiative and judgment, supporting innovative work, and maintaining open communication channels.[14] For these professionals, loyalty and commitment to the organization are built through participation.

A 1987 survey conducted by the International Association of Business Communicators (IABC) of organizations in the United States, Canada, the United Kingdom, Hong Kong, and Australia identified employee morale and motivation as the major issue for the majority of organizations in the survey. Other issues included economic competition, cost containment, productivity, technology, and consumerism.[15] Many of these areas can be impacted positively by an effective participation process involving employees in meeting organizational objectives. However, motivation remains a continuing challenge for many organizations.

Understanding motivation helps an organization integrate the involvement process more effectively. Motivation at work is strongly influenced by an individual's perception of work. Mortimer J. Adler defines two distinct forms of work: toiling and leisuring. While toiling brings financial reward and some of the comforts of life, leisuring improves the individual in mind or character.[16] Daily work for most people contains elements of both types of work. B. J. Chakiris and John J. Leach build on Adler's work in their work *The Rusting Out in America* (*ROIA*) *Studies* and explore perceptions of work in different jobs and careers.[17] They present the following definitions of work in the formal organization:

Work as Toil and Labor. A compulsory activity entered into. The activity tends to be physical in nature and when it requires mental effort, this effort is dull or repetitive.

Work as Habit or Social Prescription. A compulsory activity entered into to earn a livelihood, to fill up the day, or to acquire some of the amenities of life. The activity is somewhat skilled and tends to keep the person active. The activity does not necessarily provide growth in terms of new knowledge and increased skills. A positive organizational climate (nice boss, good benefits) may be more important to the person than the work itself.

Work as a Career Path. A compulsory activity but the person tends to have more latitude and mobility. The work itself, the challenge, and growth possibilities represent major motivators. People in this activity typically are well educated, possess above average skills, are emotionally invested in their work, and have career plans for the future.

Work as Status and Power. This is a less compulsory activity, because many people in this category are economically well-off and established in their careers.

The prospects of increasing wealth, status, and power are major motivators. Becoming a significant figure among peers and competitors motivates these people more than increasing knowledge and skill.

Chakiris and Leach also include work in a noneconomic sense that reaches beyond a job to include purposeful activities that may bring social benefit and self-development. This may include everything from community volunteer work to a night class at a local university.[17]

Work thus takes a wider perspective and defines a lifestyle and a dominant life attitude, which may or may not include participation as a major value. Many believe that people essentially are defined by their work. The familiar questions, "Where do you work?" or "What do you do?" begin countless social interactions. However, people are more realistically defined by their attitudes toward work and leisure rather than by the job description or the work itself. Understanding various work attitudes is an essential factor in implementing a successful participative process.

Motivation and interest in participation and employee involvement might be directly based on how an individual or group defines work. An employee who is accustomed to thinking of work as toil and labor may not relate to the concept of teams or problem solving groups. However, this involvement role may encourage the individual to develop a new definition of work based on greater involvement and job satisfaction.

Those who view work as habit or social prescription may join problem-solving teams because group interaction is interesting, a break from the job, or a chance to talk with other employees. For these people, the organizational climate might be improved or enhanced by a participative process such as involvement teams. While employee groups may make these individuals less dissatisfied, it may not necessarily inspire them to do better work.

Those who see work as a career plan may appreciate the opportunities for training and leadership practice that are part of the involvement process. For the career-oriented employee this individual development may be a satisfying motivator. The integration of career development into the participative process offers some powerful incentives.

Those who see work as status and power will probably appraise involvement as an opportunity to gain some influence or leadership visibility. However, successful participation is based on shared responsibility and delegation of authority. Individuals learn most about collective power and networking.

Depending on how they define work, employees may make a kind of contract with the organization. This seldom written and often unspoken contract may be the determining factor in how the individual views the organization and participation. These contracts are sometimes part of a larger life plan for the individual, influenced by factors outside the organization. The contracts are often simple: "I work here because I need the money" or "If I am not promoted within two years, I will leave this company."

Many employees do not see a career path within the organization. They are caught in dead-end jobs with routine activities. These people may have the knowledge to be more productive, but they are bored and not challenged to use their basic ability. Involvement teams can help turn these people into more productive workers with a positive attitude toward themselves and the organization.

These definitions and perceptions of work can also be placed into the hierarchy of needs discussed earlier in this chapter. These needs do affect participation.

■ Developmental Needs
  "I want to develop my talents and gain new skills."
  "I want to find out who I am and what I can do."

■ Esteem Needs
  "I want to be recognized for my accomplishments."
  "I want the respect of my co-workers."

■ Social Needs
  "I want to work as part of a top-notch team."
  "I want to work for a company that believes in people."

■ Safety/Security Needs
  "I want to know that my job is secure."
  "I want to work in an orderly, comfortable environment."

■ Basic Needs
  "I want to pay the rent and buy food for my family."
  "I want to finish my work and go home."

The level and intensity of these needs varies depending on a number of different factors including age, experience, skills, economic situation, and personal philosophy. Career development is an increasingly important factor in satisfying these needs, motivating employees, and improving organizational effectiveness.

At one time most of the theories of career development were chronological, moving through stages of growth, exploration, establishment, maintenance, and decline. For some career specialists, this approach is often limiting. The work of innovative career and developmental consultants points to a more positive and flexible career path based on options for constant renewal, learning, and growth. Maintenance and routine work can be countered with different kinds of work and with a broader definition of work and leisure. Stages of exploration and individual growth can be enhanced through employee involvement and participation.

One research study focused on team members' perception of participation and its effects on related organizational communication variables. Results showed that participation has a positive effect on perceived individual power/influence and on communication with superiors. In this study, participation did not significantly affect perceptions of advancement, belonging, or tangible rewards.[18] This is certainly an area that requires further research.

The Development Process

The involvement process works on three levels: individual development, group development, and organizational development. Individual development is based on skill training as well as opportunities for practice and feedback on performance. As individuals learn and apply problem-solving techniques, they increase organizational efficiency, productivity, and service. The teams also concentrate on monitoring and preventing problems. As the group works together, they understand more about cooperation and teamwork throughout the organization. Teams also recognize the interdependence of all parts of the organization. Staff development and improved supervision can result from the participative process. Employees develop a greater respect for leadership and understand the necessity for many of the procedures and practices of the organization. The model (Figure 1.1) focuses on the benefits of a participative process for the individual and the organization.

This does not always mean that participation brings development on the individual, group, and organizational levels. In some cases where the participative process has not succeeded, programs were pushed as a tool to increase productivity and profits without an equal amount of emphasis on the critical role the individual and the group play in the total process. A survey of some of the first organizations to adopt quality circles in the United States showed that highly successful programs stress people-building objectives in addition to quality and productivity goals.[19]

Productivity begins with committed people. The organization has to be willing to share some information and power with employees in return for commitment and productivity. Committed people will make more demands on management and the organization. These employees are more willing to challenge traditional methods that no longer seem appropriate. They are also less willing to stay with routine jobs. These people will ask for respect and recognition within the organizational system. Yet their energy, skills, and commitment through involvement processes such as quality circles, employee involvement groups, and improvement teams can bring great rewards to the organization, creating a synergy that is greater than any individual person.

T. J. Peters and R. H. Waterman describe excellent companies in terms of their ability to motivate and inspire the average employee, "These institutions create environments in which people can blossom, develop self-esteem, and otherwise be excited participants in the business and in society as a whole."[20] The process of participation begins with a realization of need and opportunity as well as a recognition of an interdependent relationship—individual, group, and organizational. What organization would not want to have employees who were "excited participants in the business"? The strength of the organization is still the individual employee committed to organizational values and ready to take responsibility for helping to reach organizational goals.

FIGURE 1.1

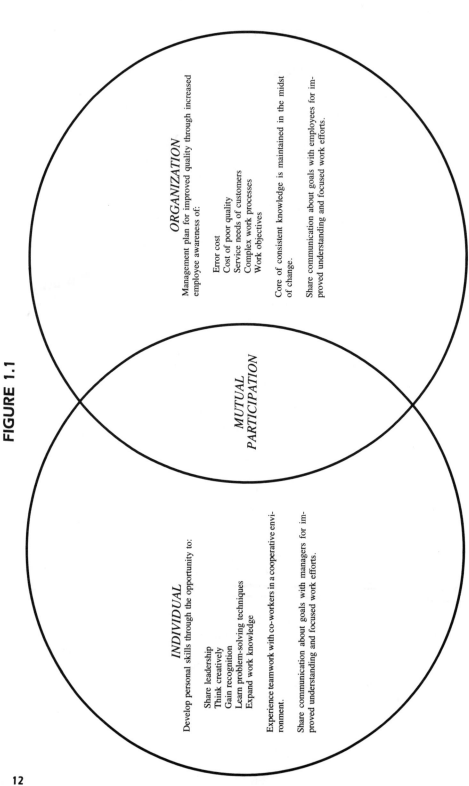

INDIVIDUAL
Develop personal skills through the opportunity to:

Share leadership
Think creatively
Gain recognition
Learn problem-solving techniques
Expand work knowledge

Experience teamwork with co-workers in a cooperative environment.

Share communication about goals with managers for improved understanding and focused work efforts.

MUTUAL PARTICIPATION

ORGANIZATION
Management plan for improved quality through increased employee awareness of:

Error cost
Cost of poor quality
Service needs of customers
Complex work processes
Work objectives

Core of consistent knowledge is maintained in the midst of change.

Share communication about goals with employees for improved understanding and focused work efforts.

References

1. Argyris, Chris. *Integrating the Individual and the Organization*. New York: John Wiley & Sons, 1964.

2. Likert, Rensis. *The Human Organization: Its Management and Value*. New York: McGraw-Hill Book Co., 1967.

3. McGregor, Douglas. *The Human Side of Enterprise*. New York: McGraw-Hill Book Co., 1960.

4. Ouchi, William G. *Theory Z*. Reading, MA: Addison-Wesley Publishing Co., 1981.

5. Herzberg, Frederick. *Work and the Nature of Man*. New York: Thomas Crowell Co., 1966.

6. Maslow, A. H. *Motivation and Personality*. New York: Harper & Row, 1954.

7. Levine, Herminezagat. "The Squeeze on Middle Management." *Personnel* 63, No. 1 (Jan. 1986): 62–69.

8. Ishikawa, Kaoru. *Guide to Quality Control*. Tokyo, Japan: Asian Productivity Organization, 1976.

9. Deming, William Edwards. *Elementary Principles of the Statistical Control of Quality* 2d ed. Tokyo, Japan: Nippon Kagaku Gijutsu Remmei, 1952.

10. Juran, J. M. *Quality Control Handbook* 3d ed. New York: McGraw-Hill Book Co., 1974.

11. Olson, James E. "The State of Quality in the U.S. Today: James E. Olson on Quality, Cost, and Customer Satisfaction." *Quality Progress* 18, No. 7 (July 1985): 32–36.

12. Richards, Bob. "White Collar Quality Circles and Productivity." *Training and Development Journal* 38, No. 10 (Oct. 1984): 92–98.

13. Lawler, Edward E. III. "Education, Management Style, and Organizational Effectiveness." *Personnel Psychology* 38, No. 1 (Spring 1985): 1–26.

14. Kelley, Robert E. *The Gold Collar Worker: Harnessing the Brainpower of the New Workforce*. Reading, MA: Addison-Wesley Publishing Co., 1985.

15. International Association of Business Communicators Foundation "Profile 87." San Francisco: IABC Foundation, 1987.

16. Adler, Mortimer J. *A Vision of the Future: Twelve Ideas for a Better Life and a Better Society*. New York: Macmillan, 1984.

17. Leach, John J., and B. J. Chakiris. *The Rusting Out in America (ROIA) Studies*. Chicago, IL: B. J. Chakiris Corporation, 1985. Leach, John J. and B. J. Chakiris. "The Future of Jobs, Work and Careers" American Society of Training and Development National Conference, Atlanta, 1987.

18. Elvine, Jane P. "Communication in Quality Circles: Members Perceptions of Their Participation and Its Effects on Related Organizational Communication Variables." *Group and Organizational Studies* 10, No. 4 (Dec. 1985): 479–507.

19. Cole, Robert E., and Dennis S. Tachiki. "Forging Institutional Links: Making Quality Circles Work in the U.S." *National Productivity Review* 3, No. 4 (Autumn 1984): 417–29.

20. Peters, T. J., and R. H. Waterman. *In Search of Excellence*. New York: Harper & Row, 1982.

CHAPTER 2

Introducing the Participative Process into the Organization

Introducing any change into an organization is a challenging process. Whether the words are written or spoken, there are familiar phrases used to stifle new ideas and discourage excessive innovation: "That's a great idea, but . . ." or "I believe in this, but . . ." These phrases are all too familiar to those who have tried to introduce change into traditional organizations. The following statements are common responses to proposals for participation and employee involvement:

- "Participation is a good idea, but it will never work in this organization."

- "Participation is a good idea, but what will managers do if employees start making all the decisions?"

- "Participation is a good idea, but it will disrupt our procedures. Everything is working fine now."

- "Participation is a good idea, but it's too much trouble to administer. We don't have time for that."

- "Participation is a good idea, but it takes employees away from their real work."

In introducing a process such as employee involvement or quality teams, there may be an immediate attempt to change an entire organization to a more participative style. R. M. Kanter refers to the dilemma of *participation-by-command* and explains this as "something the top orders the middle to do for the bottom."[1] Forced change can create resistance and conflict.[2] People should be involved in planning for change. Managers and employees must understand the goals and benefits realistically. Working on a small scale with supportive departments is often a more practical approach for introducing participation and employee involvement.

There are varying views on how much change an organizational culture must make to implement the participative process effectively. There may be some impact in specific areas, but it is unlikely the entire organization can be changed easily. Major change in organizational culture is a slow process requiring from three to seven years in most organizations. Some change may occur in the organization as a result of a participative process, such as quality teams, but this is more often an individual change relating to employees, supervisors, and managers who have been involved directly in the participative process. Visualizing the process of change helps in undertanding the complex dimensions that are involved in any change process.[3]

The process of implementing participation or employee involvement involves coordination that recognizes the political, social, and economic structure of the organization. The most successful programs adapt and integrate into already existing processes and procedures. The following participative concepts help reinforce employee responsibility and the current leadership role of the supervisor:

- The person who knows the job best is the person who does that job.

- Employees should have access to information that can help them do their job better.

- Supervisors can facilitate teamwork and increased productivity through group problem solving in their department.

- Employees can apply an understanding of the basic principles of information gathering, analysis, and problem solving to increase their efficiency on the job.

These are not new or revolutionary concepts. Many effective supervisors and managers recognize and practice these concepts. However, even with the best intentions, these concepts often have not been used because of the lack of an organized, participative approach that includes planning, training, monitoring, and evaluation.

In effective organizations, management deals with the process of change. Organizations must be in a constant process of development and renewal.[4] This requires proactive management, creative leadership, and planned change that involves employees and uses communication and effective problem solving. The participative organization is an open organization characterized by *unity* in planning and mission; *internal responsiveness* in human relations, problem solving, and organizational development; and *external responsiveness* in relation to profitability and innovation in the marketplace and social responsibility in the community and the world.[5]

The following steps outline a plan for introducing participative processes such as employee involvement, quality circles, and improvement teams into an organization. This process may occur within one department, section, division, or an entire organization. There may be additional steps in some organizations, or steps may be combined. The activities listed below can structure the orientation and pilot implementation of the participative process in many organizations.

- Recognizing need or opportunity
- Defining objectives and goals
- Establishing roles and responsibilities
- Planning for implementation

■ Training and skills development

■ Establishing baseline data

■ Providing information and feedback

■ Implementing action

■ Evaluating results

Some organizations may start a few employee involvement groups with little time spent in orientation or planning. Sometimes this works, but in most cases the groups soon flounder and fail. The participative process requires preparation and a basic supporting structure for guidance, feedback, and evaluation. The steps listed on the pages that follow describe an effective approach to introducing participative concepts into most organizations. The process begins with recognition of need or opportunity.

Recognizing Need or Opportunity

Needs, caused by increased errors, missed deadlines, or machinery that is not operating properly, are obvious; other needs related to work flow, outdated filing systems, or employee motivation may not be so obvious. In some cases, needs and opportunities are not recognized immediately, but become more evident as employees and managers begin to gather information and analyze problems. Recognizing a particular need or opportunity often begins the initiation of a participative process, but the process should continue to reveal needs and opportunities related to quality, productivity, and work efficiency. This cycle establishes the monitoring and feedback system that documents and supports the process for senior management and for employees. It is important to identify the initial need or opportunity that brings participative practices and concepts into a specific organization. The following questions are useful in assessing initial need or opportunity:

■ With what individual or group does the need or opportunity originate?

■ How does the need or opportunity relate to current organizational objectives, goals, and values?

■ How many people does this need or opportunity affect?

■ At what levels of the organization is this need or opportunity recognized?

■ What are the potential costs and benefits involved in dealing with this need or opportunity?

Establishing the origin of the participative idea helps in understanding motivators and assessing support. Someone may suggest quality teams or an employee involvement program that might help in a particular area. Perhaps a manager will decide to hold regular meetings with employees to discuss problems with departmental efficiency. In another case, a senior executive may want to put participative concepts into practice to increase cost savings and profitability. Improving employee morale or developing job training may also prompt a recognition of a need or opportunity. While many needs come from management initiative, the attitude and behavior of employees may also indicate an opportunity for change or development. The source of the impetus and enthusiasm for participation should be identified and clearly understood. Is this motivation shared by few people, or is there wide interest among managers and employees across several departments or divisions?

Employees may or may not recognize the potential benefits of the participative process immediately. Some employees are anxious to be more involved with problem solving in the workplace. Others are not as eager to accept this opportunity. Response to the participative process is often dependent on the ability and attitude of the workers. Do they possess the skills and knowledge necessary to solve work-related problems? Are the majority of employees sufficiently committed to the organization to take responsibility and set goals for improving their productivity?

Before considering any employee involvement, the relationship of participation to current organizational activities should be explored. How closely does the concept of participation link with existing management practices? Does employee involvement match organizational values and priorities? The answers to these questions help to make a realistic assessment of environment and readiness.

Introduction of the participative process should be based on real needs or opportunities rather than a quirk or a temporary call for innovation or assistance. Generally, the process should not be implemented in a time of crisis, but at a time when there is a genuine and shared interest in improving an organization that already is working well. However, there are some situations when employee groups can assist the organization in difficult times. For example, major organizational changes such as mergers or reorganizations may be facilitated by employee teams focusing on the integration of departmental functions. Yet the participative process cannot be considered a quick fix for serious organizational problems.

The best environment for success is one in which senior managers and supervisors recognize the need or opportunity and begin the participative process with respect for the recognition of the skills and knowledge of employees. Managers must have a realistic expectation of results from participation, as well. Employees should enter the process with accurate information and orientation. If employees understand management's needs and expectations they can make more effective contributions.

The next step is to decide how the participative process can be adapted to fit into the existing organizational structure. This means carefully defining goals based on current organization priorities and directions.

Defining Objectives and Goals

After the need or opportunity is recognized, an executive group including key managers and external resource persons should meet to define overall objectives for the participative process. This meeting often begins with an orientation or overview of the participative process followed by discussion and application to the specific organization. A senior executive usually leads the discussion session. Although the discussion may be confidential, the content should be documented in minutes and major ideas should be displayed on flip charts for group reference.

Specific goal definitions guide planning by focusing on items such as organizational impact, priority needs, expected results, action steps, and time frames. Goals fall into two basic categories: (1) those related to cost savings, including productivity, quality improvement, and error reduction; and (2) those focused on employee development, such as leadership, self-confidence, ability to work as a team, and increased knowledge of organizational priorities and procedures. All initial management goals should be considered in both current and strategic terms. The participative process takes anywhere from six months to a year to move through the cycle of training and the first completed projects. While some progress toward goals may be evident early in the process, many results are strategic, that is slow-developing for long-term benefits. Maximum cost-to-savings ratios, for example, are often reached only after three or four years of operation.

The most realistic goals are those that are anchored within the current organizational system and supported by management. Successful participative goals apply the following developmental principles:

- Integration into the present organizational structure

- Reinforcement of current organizational priorities

- Network of management support

- Orientation and training for employees and management

- Voluntary participation and individual commitment

- Continual monitoring and evaluation with adequate communication and feedback cycles

Participation does not happen in a few weeks or months. The process requires a continuing commitment from management. This goes beyond the approval of a proposal or the time spent in planning meetings or training sessions. This commitment is an attitude and a management style that reinforces participative concepts. Integration of overall objectives and specific goals is an important part of establishing and maintaining management support.

Organizations may vary in their priority objectives. In one organization, which has expanded from a small "family" to a more complex, decentralized structure, the executive group set an overriding objective to increase employee self-esteem through involvement and recognition of quality teams. Other organizations may concentrate on the direct cost savings or quality improvement from their employee involvement groups. Many organizations choose specific goals that combine both task and people dimensions of any participative process.

The following list presents some management priorities and needs in a participative program:

- Reduce errors and enhance quality

- Improve overall productivity

- Increase employee involvement

- Increase employee motivation

- Inspire more effective teamwork

- Improve communication

- Encourage creative thinking

- Enhance problem-solving capability

- Increase a quality service attitude

- Develop a more effective manager/employee relationship

- Recognize employee contributions to the organization

- Promote personal growth

- Develop leadership

The executive group should establish some basic objectives. Then goals are developed, prioritized, and measurement criteria are determined. The next step is to establish specific roles and responsibilities for the introduction and pilot implementation of the participative process.

Establishing Roles and Responsibilities

One of the most important roles is held by the individual or department sponsoring the participative process. This may be the president of the company or a senior executive. It should be someone who is respected by people in the organization and who has the power to make strategic decisions and bring financial and political support to the process. The sponsor may also be a specific department such as quality assurance or human resources. Whether the program is sponsored by an individual or a department, several key questions must be answered in order to integrate this pivotal role:

- What does the sponsoring person, group, or department expect as a result of the participative process?

- What role will the sponsor play in the total process? How actively will the sponsor be involved in group operation and administration?

- Who will ultimately be responsible for results?

The actual coordinator of the program within the organization—usually someone from operations, human resources, quality control, or a related area—plays the most crucial operational role. The coordinator directs and documents the process, and does a substantial amount of marketing to both management and employees. This position requires someone who can communicate effectively with people throughout the organization. The coordinator must be aware of the day-to-day operations of the participative process. To enhance the credibility and effectiveness of the process, the coordinator should also be someone who can influence decision making, budget, and procedures for the participative process. Coordinators may assume this position as a part-time responsibility in addition to other job functions. However, managing a successful process in a large organization may be a full-time responsibility.

Managers and senior executives must have a role in introducing employee involvement into the organization in order to integrate the participative process into the organizational system and to recognize current management structure and power bases. Any participative process should recognize the existing power structure in both the formal and informal networks of the organization. An understanding of decision-making procedures and patterns helps to make this integration. Is decision making centralized or decentralized? Who are the people who can influence decisions? Senior executives, strategic managers, and influential employees may represent the beliefs and values of the organization in a visible and articulate way. These key people can connect the participative process to the existing organizational culture.

In order to establish a base of support from top management and other key people in the organization, the formation of an advisory group or steering committee should be one of the first steps in identifying roles. The terms *steering committee* and *advisory group* are often used interchangeably. However, the concept of "steering" bothers some experts. They prefer to use the terms *advisory* or *task force*. Whatever the title, this advisory group has substantial responsibility for establishing structure and direction, especially in the beginning of the process. This does not mean that the steering committee or advisory group should be discontinued after the process is in operation. This advisory group is part of the permanent structure of a participative process. Large organizations may have several steering committees in different departments or divisions. Because of the influence of this advisory group, it is important to establish clear guidelines for roles and responsibilities. The following questions should be answered early in the planning discussions:

- How large should the advisory group be? Who should be included?

- Should all membership on the advisory group be rotated or should there be some permanent members?

- Will more than one advisory group be required as the process expands? How will this advisory group be structured?

- What commitment (time, resources, support) is expected from advisory group members?

- What administrative authority does the advisory group have?

Table 2.1 is a section from a policy and procedures manual for a quality team program in a major financial institution that describes the role and responsibility of a steering committee. This particular organization has several steering committees in different departments.

Individual managers play a significant role in the introduction and operation of the participative process. Management support can mean the difference between group success or failure. The role and responsibility of management are outlined in this section from a participative policy manual (Table 2.2). Many of these are

TABLE 2.1

Policy Manual
Steering Committee

The steering committee consists of representatives from General Banking Services Operations (GBS Operations) and quality assurance personnel designated by the committee. The chairperson is the operating general manager and members include assistant operating general managers, three division managers, three team leaders, three facilitators, quality assurance personnel, and the GBS Operations training coordinator for quality teams.

Voting members include the assistant operating general managers, division managers, team leaders, and facilitators. The nonvoting members include the chairperson, quality assurance personnel, and the GBS Operations training coordinator for quality teams. The division managers, facilitators, and team leaders will be replaced every six months on a rotating basis.

The chairperson reports progress on a quarterly basis to the corporate office. Decisions are reached through the participative process. A majority of members must be present to make a decision.

Steering committee members meet regularly. The chairperson or any cochairperson has the authority to call committee meetings as appropriate. The co-chairperson will be appointed by the chairperson and will be an assistant operating general manager.

Steering committee members may have substitutes attend meetings. In such cases, prior notice is given to the chairperson and is subject to the chairperson's approval. The substitute may not vote. If an issue is scheduled for a vote, a written proxy may be sent to the meeting and a simple majority will rule.

The primary functions of the steering committee are:

- Declare general objectives for quality teams, such as quality improvement, cost reduction, and improved communication.

- Limit issues to those within the charter of quality teams.

- Control the rate of team implementation.

- Determine how expenses will be allocated.

- Arrange for necessary training for leaders and facilitators.

- Encourage growth of team activities to encompass all relevant areas of operations.

- Provide guidelines for the measurement of team activities and monitor cost effectiveness and progress.

- Establish appropriate rewards and recognitions.

- Promote and initiate management teams.

- Provide all division managers and facilitators with minutes of steering committee meetings.

TABLE 2.2

Policy Manual
Management Responsibility

Management responsibilities in the participative process include the following:

- Encouraging formation of employee problem-solving groups.

- Authorizing weekly meetings and encouraging members to attend.

- Allowing member representatives to attend meetings of other groups when working on joint projects.

- Authorizing group leader candidates to participate in leader training.

- Consulting with the leader and facilitator on a quarterly basis to ensure development of the group.

- Determining the effectiveness of the leader and offering appropriate support.

- Providing adequate meeting areas, equipment, and supplies.

- Authorizing selective leader/member involvement at outside conferences.

- Supporting group activities in speeches and presentations.

- Including employee group activities as part of divisional goals and including group issues in divisional activity reports.

- Respecting the autonomy of employee groups.

- Encouraging management presentations as a vital aspect of group activities, and providing communication, motivation, and recognition.

- Responding expeditiously to group requests and recommendations, and providing a detailed explanation for recommendations that cannot be implemented.

- Implementing approved group recommendations with minimum delay.

- Encouraging management groups.

a part of the standard responsibilities for managing people and resources and supporting employee development.

After the general roles and responsibilities are outlined, the next step is to plan for introduction and implementation of the participative process.

Planning for Implementation

The coordinator, advisory committee, and respresentative managers accept some responsibility for planning and supporting the introduction and implementation of pilot groups in specific departments. While some members of these groups may be enthusiastic, and others skeptical, they agree at this point to at least test the process through the pilot groups. Their initial role is often direct involvement in planning for implementation.

One of the first aspects of planning is to ask strategic questions that will guide and structure the participative process. After these questions are answered, formal policies and procedures can be developed.

Implementation Checklist

Communication

■ How will members of the advisory committee receive information about groups?

■ How will information be reported to the sponsoring individual or department?

■ How will groups access organizational records and files? What records and files will be available to groups? What records will not be available?

■ How will groups share information and resources with other groups?

Decision Making

■ What is the scope of power and authority in individual employee teams?

■ How will decisions be made on implementation of group proposals and projects?

■ How will conflicts and disagreements among groups, leaders, or facilitators be mediated and resolved?

■ How will decisions be made regarding formation of new teams and status of inactive groups?

Evaluation

■ What criteria will be used to evaluate the success of the participative process?

■ What are the standards for the approval and implementation of projects?

■ How will the progress and development of groups be monitored?

■ Who will be responsible for evaluation?

Resources

■ What internal resources are available? What external resources will be required (consultants, training materials)?

■ How much company time will be used for information gathering, training, and group meetings? How much time will employees spend on team projects? How much time will be required from supervisors and managers?

■ What organizational resources (facilities, equipment, supplies) will be available for the groups?

Finances

- What are the overall cost estimates of implementing the process? What are the direct and indirect costs?

- Which budgets will cover expenses such as outside resources, training materials, and printing?

- What funds are available in the current budget? What funds will be required in future budgets to maintain the process?

- What is a reasonable expectation of the cost-to-savings ratio in the first year of operation?

Orientation and Pilot

- How will employees be informed about the process (discussion meetings, printed materials, video, speeches)?

- How will the call for volunteers be handled?

- What role will the line supervisor play in initial orientation?

- How will the pilot groups be chosen?

Although this checklist does not include all the questions that might arise, the major areas for discussion are indicated. The planning group may spend a substantial amount of time sorting out the answers to these questions. However, thorough discussion and planning at this stage can help prevent difficulties later.

The planning group needs to assess some of the current organizational attitudes toward participation. One useful tool in understanding climate and readiness is the *force field analysis.* This is an assessment of the supporting and opposing factors that could affect the participative process positively or negatively. The relative strength of these forces can also be established by estimating influence, resources, and intensity of each factor on a numerical scale. A simple force field analysis might look like this:

Supporting Forces	*Restraining Forces*
president's commitment	little involvement of middle managers
employee interest	uncertainty about change
need for some improvement in productivity	lack of information about participation

This visualization allows the planning group to see areas of support and areas of potential resistance affecting implementation of the participative process. Once significant forces are recognized and evaluated, the supporting forces can be used and restraining forces reduced to facilitate the implementation of the participative process. While this analysis may include some speculation and instinct, it is also based on direct observation and experience of the planning group.

An organizational chart may also give another perspective of support and resistance within the organization, pointing to the most positive sections for implementation and illustrating the pattern of support within the traditional organizational hierarchy. The participative process sometimes has strong support from senior management and involves many employees, but leaves middle managers out of the process. The role of middle managers must also be considered.

If the union is part of the organization, its position should also be considered an influencing factor. Attempts to improve productivity and increase employee involvement may be met with suspicion from the union if union leaders or representatives are not informed and involved in the initial planning. Areas that generally are determined to be inappropriate for team discussion and action are personnel matters and grievances, including wages and salaries, benefits, disciplinary policies, employment policies, termination policies, and individual personalities. If union leaders see participation as a process that can improve the overall quality of work life for employees and are included in the planning process, the union can be a positive supporting force.

Other individuals or groups who play a role in the development and maintenance of organizational culture should also be considered. T. Deal and A. A. Kennedy list some of these people as *storytellers,* who interpret what goes on in the organization; *priests,* who are guardians of the culture's values; *whisperers,* who may influence leaders behind the scenes, and the *cabals,* groups of two or more who secretly join to accomplish some common purpose.[6] These people may be in key leadership positions or serve as powerful opinion leaders.

To be effective in planning and decision making, the planning group should analyze potential positive and negative influences. Observation is one of the simplest ways to gather information about the culture and informal organizational behavior and norms. Observations may be made in several areas including work habits, group cohesiveness, and decision-making procedures. Recognizing work habits is one method of assessing group norms and routine behaviors that structure work life and work functions. The following are some basic questions relating to work patterns:

- Is the functional work process integrated into group activity or is the pattern based on independent work?

- What are the seasonal peaks and valleys of work volume? What are the daily peaks and valleys of work volume? When do deadlines occur?

- What resources are available to cover jobs?

- How does the physical environment and layout of the office or plant affect work flow?

■ What type of contact do employees have with each other and with their supervisor during an average workday?

■ Do employees have any discretionary time?

There are problems in not recognizing or in violating established organizational work habits. Norms related to time are especially significant. A flexible work schedule can affect meeting hours. Employees may feel inconvenienced if they have to come early or stay late. Split shift groups have trouble getting all members to regular meetings. Customer contact employees often are not able to leave their area for a meeting. All of these circumstances and time procedures can affect the participative process in a particular department.

The planning group should also consider how participation can affect employee motivation in these areas. The current sense of teamwork and group cohesiveness should be evaluated. Are there underlying conflicts or problems that could prevent teamwork? Are certain cliques or subgroups evident in particular departments? What are the demographic variations within particular departments? What do employees talk about when they are together? Do employees socialize as a group? Employee participation in current activities such as committees, project teams, task forces, and even company sports teams may be helpful in creating a cooperative participative atmosphere in which people learn to work together.

An employee's current level of involvement in decision making is also an important area to assess. Do employees make any decisions related to the work in their department? How actively do employees participate in departmental meetings and other opportunities for input in decision making? Does the organization inform employees about organizational policies and procedures so that employees can make effective decisions? How can the participative process complement divisional structure and procedures?

Information from observation and experience provides insight into how the participative process can be integrated into the current organizational system. The next action of the planning group is to establish objectives and specific goals. After objectives and goals have been developed, initial orientation and training for employees, supervisors, and managers begin the actual implementation cycle.

Training and Skill Development

Training does not always have to occur in a formal situation or a classroom. It can happen in a management meeting or in a conversation between a leader and a facilitator. In the broadest definition, training for participation occurs at several levels within the organization:

■ Coordinator training

■ Management orientation

■ General orientation for all employees

- Management training
- Leader and facilitator training
- Group member training
- Advanced leader and facilitator training
- Advanced problem-solving training for groups
- Organizational resource centers
- Consultation by coordinator, facilitator, leader, or outside resource

Training is a requirement throughout the participative process, and advanced training is one response to this continuing need. An aspect of training that is sometimes neglected is the orientation for management and employees. Everyone in the organization should get some initial orientation on participative concepts. Employee orientation increases awareness of participative concepts, conveys basic information on the process, and encourages volunteers for groups. The management orientation, related to organizational goals and objectives, shows how the process fits into current structure and procedures, and outlines opportunities for teams in particular departments. Managers and supervisors should authorize participative groups in their areas. In these orientations, training is meant to inform and encourage participation at all levels of the organization.

The core of training for participation is often related to basic problem-solving skills including information gathering, analysis, and application. This training is usually brought into the organization by one of the following approaches:

The Package Approach. The coordinator attends a training institute or certification course outside the organization and returns to the organization to establish this training procedure. Or, the coordinator purchases a package program from a consulting firm or training facility and conducts the training based on the materials in the package, which may include workbooks and media support.

The Expert Approach. An external resource person comes into the organization for a limited period of time and does the initial training and/or conducts train-the-trainer sessions. The training program is established with the philosophy and practices of the expert.

The Team Approach. The coordinator and key managers work as a task force with an external resource person to establish appropriate training and procedures. Basic training programs are often customized to meet specific organizational needs. The coordinator and the external resource person present the initial training. The task force also develops a feedback and monitoring system for training and development needs.

The role of the training coordinator varies with each approach. The package approach puts the coordinator in the position of internal resource person and trainer. The internal coordinator guides the organization in planning, training, implementing, and evaluating the participative process. In the package approach the coordinator also assumes substantial responsibility for training.

There are some disadvantages to using only internal resources for start-up training. The internal coordinator may make decisions based on the political and economic implications of participation within the organization. The coordinator may not always have the power necessary to establish the process in particular departments. Perhaps the coordinator has many specific management skills but no training or experience in facilitating all aspects of the participative process, especially in collecting data and giving feedback. In some cases, the internal coordinator may have other responsibilities within the organization, that limit administration of the participative process to a part-time activity.

The expert approach involves the assistance of an external resource person. This may be a consultant, a coordinator from another company in the same industry, a professor from a local university, or a professional from a trade group or association. Often the external resource person comes into the organization for a short time to do initial training and to establish the process. Once the process is established, this external expert moves to another client, but has occasional follow-up contact with the organization. There are advantages to bringing in an expert with experience in implementing the participative process with a variety of organizations. The expertise and energy of this person can provide a strong start-up for the organization. The outside person is also more objective and unbiased in working through the politics of the organization.

Exit procedures should be established. Unless the external resource has trained others to continue the process, the initial enthusiasm may be lost in later confusion. In some cases, problems with group development and operational procedures do not surface until after the external person has left the system. Sometimes the training manuals and workbooks left behind do not answer the questions that may come up in the day-to-day functioning of the participative process. Training is more than information resources. Continued guidance through analysis, application, and practice makes the information practical in a group situation. If this internal guidance system has not been developed, the initial training may not be successful in maintaining team development. Eventually participative training can be integrated into the management system, but in the first year some additional external support may be needed, especially for monitoring results and establishing information needs.

Another way to work with an outside professional is to establish a task force or working team that will coordinate internal and external resources. The external resource person trains the internal coordinator to develop the skills necessary to implement and maintain the total participative process. The external person also serves as a guide for the internal coordinator as needed. This cooperative relationship may exist over an extended period of time. The external resource works within the organization as part of an internal team, reducing any uneasiness that might be felt toward an outsider.

This approach may have some pitfalls if the internal coordinator depends too heavily on the external resource person and does not develop individual judgment and skills. The team approach also takes a longer time because of the emphasis

TABLE 2.3

Sample Training Plan

Week	Activity
5/4	Facilitator training
5/11	Management overview
6/1	Steering committee formed Initial meeting
6/8	Selection of supervisors for leader training
6/15	Three-day training for leaders
6/22	Orientation for sections
6/29	Orientation for sections
7/6	Three-day leader training (additional leaders)
7/13	Selection of sections for pilot teams
7/20	Four pilot teams begin training
8/24	Four pilot teams complete training
9/14	Four additional teams begin to receive training
10/19	Four additional teams complete training
10/26	Four pilot teams near completion of first projects
1/11	Four additional teams near completion of first projects

on information gathering, group analysis, and planning. However, the team approach is usually more successful because of the strength of internal and external coordination, and the development and training that occurs on both an individual and a group level during the implementation process.

Whatever training approach is chosen, the training sequence and coordination must be planned carefully. A typical training plan (Table 2.3) documents the sequence from initial orientation and training to the completion of the first team projects.

The planning group must establish the training program that has the greatest probability of success in meeting the organizational objectives. One of the most critical decisions at this point is the selection of the department or area for the first pilot teams and the choice of people who will be in the initial training groups. The people who might be included in the initial training group are members of the human resource or training staff who will later serve as facilitators, senior managers who want more exposure to the program, and supervisors who will lead and train the first pilot teams.

The actual areas or sections for the pilot groups should be chosen strategically. The following characteristics can increase the probability of success:

- High morale and sense of teamwork

- Frequent opportunities for working together in a group to accomplish departmental goals

- One department that can serve as a model for other departments

- Enthusiastic and capable supervisors who can lead the team through start-up, training, and problem solving

- Employees who have a high success rate on other types of projects and activities

The number of pilot groups varies depending on the interest and resources within the organization. Some organizations have only one or two pilot groups, while others have ten or more. The number of initial teams should not be too large. This training experience must be supported and monitored carefully to evaluate the effectiveness of initial training and to determine additional training needs.

Establishing Baseline Data

To monitor the impact of training and group development effectively, baseline data should be established. This information documents where the organization is as the participative process begins. Baseline data may come from attitude surveys, questionnaires, individual interviews and focus groups, production records, customer complaints, error rates, and summary data such as employee turnover and absenteeism. Baseline data reveal information such as the following:

- Level of employee awareness or recognition of quality and productivity

- Attitudes and expectations of management in relation to the participative process

- Organizational climate and culture including values, behavior, and group norms

- Amount of employee involvement in problem solving and decision making

- Employee motivation factors

- Productivity levels

- Employees' job-related knowledge

- Training needs and requirements

- Employee and manager perception of problem and opportunity areas

This information provides realistic criteria and guidelines for monitoring and evaluation. Progress can be documented accurately in critical areas of organizational development over a period of time.

One instrument that has been useful in generating valuable baseline data for strategic planning and organizational development is the *Human Resource Audit*. This audit also provides data in areas such as supervision, communication, productivity, motivation, and decision making. The audit has been used extensively in service industries and is especially useful as an initial benchmark and later as a monitoring tool in the participative process.[7]

The audit attempts to meet the specific information requirements of senior executives and managers. Before the audit is administered, managers are asked to complete a checklist of their major needs.

Priority Needs

_____ Identify organizational strengths, weaknesses, and challenges.

_____ Assess organizational communication effectiveness.

_____ Learn how employees view their personal productivity.

_____ Understand what motivates employees to do their best work.

_____ Encourage giving and receiving feedback.

_____ Promote effective utilization of people.

_____ Make the organization more responsive to customers' needs.

_____ Help the organization become more responsive to employees' needs.

_____ Challenge people to contribute their ideas to the organization.

_____ Promote team leadership at the middle management level.

_____ Develop leadership skills at the supervisory management level.

_____ Obtain employee recommendations on productivity and quality.

_____ Improve overall organizational performance.

Many of these needs relate to the previous list of objectives for the participative process. This integration of needs is beneficial in focusing information gathering efforts.

The Human Resource Audit contains 114 questions related to the following areas:

■ Present job

■ Supervisor, work group, and department

■ The organization, its reward system, and its structure

■ The performance and effectiveness of the organization

A sample page from the Human Resource Audit is shown (Table 2.4). The questions refer to one's present job. Note question number 22 on employee percep-

TABLE 2.4

	Circle One			
The statements in this section refer to your present job.	Strongly Disagree	Disagree	Agree	Strongly Agree
1. The amount of work I'm expected to do is fair and reasonable.	1	2	8	4	1
2. I do the same things over and over again on my job.	1	2	3	4	2
3. When a problem comes up on my job, I am encouraged to solve it on my own.	1	2	3	4	3
4. My job is a challenge to me.	1	2	3	4	4
5. There is a lot of uncertainty and ambiguity regarding what I'm supposed to do on my job.	1	2	3	4	5
6. My job is varied and rarely routine.	1	2	3	4	6
7. I experience a high level of stress due to the pressure of my work.	1	2	3	4	7
8. I have the freedom to decide the best way to get my job done.	1	2	3	4	8
9. My job allows me to use a variety of my skills and abilities.	1	2	3	4	9
10. Even minor changes in the way I do my job must be approved by a supervisor.	1	2	3	4	10
11. Given my workload, it is possible for me to finish my job "on schedule."	1	2	3	4	11
12. I know what is expected of me on the job.	1	2	3	4	12
13. My job challenges me to be creative.	1	2	3	4	13
14. I understand how my job fits into this organization.	1	2	3	4	14
15. I get to do many different things on my job.	1	2	3	4	15
16. My job allows me to be innovative in finding ways to do it better.	1	2	3	4	16
17. I have a clear idea of what my responsibilities are on my job.	1	2	3	4	17
18. There is sufficient time for me to do my job the way I think it should be done.	1	2	3	4	18
19. The job I hold is too easy for someone with my background and experience.	1	2	3	4	19
20. I am given the opportunity to plan how my work should be carried out.	1	2	3	4	20
21. I would continue working for this organization even if I could get a slightly better paying job with another employer.	1	2	3	4	21

22. Considering your present potential, to what degree (%) do you feel you are productive in your job? Circle one.

    1—90–100%   2—80–90%   3—70–80%   4—below 70%

tion of current productivity. The answers to this question generally show that employees themselves admit that they are often only moderately productive on the job. They may blame supervisors, procedures, or equipment for their lack of productivity. The results of this question and others on the audit help employees focus on quality and productivity in terms of their jobs and their responsibility.

The responses to questions on the audit provide an assessment of current decision-making patterns and job responsibilities as well as innovation and flexibility in the workplace. The Human Resource Audit also includes some specific questions related to individual motivation and productivity on the job (Table 2.5).

The most frequent answers often deal with recognition, responsibility, and salary. While participation does not affect salary levels directly, it can be used to motivate individuals and improve productivity.

Employee perception of organizational priorities is also assessed in the audit (Table 2.6). Sometimes these perceptions differ substantially from those of management. Clear understanding of organizational priorities is essential in structuring an appropriate participative process.

The audit also encourages employee comments with open-ended questions, such as listing improvements in three categories that would make the organization more effective or a better place to work. The categories are: (1) improvements regarding working conditions and relationships; (2) improvements regarding the quality of products or services offered; and (3) improvements regarding productivity and efficiency.

TABLE 2.5

23. In your present job, to what extent do each of the following motivate you to do your best work?

Circle one number for each lettered item.

		To great extent	To moderate extent	To small extent	Not at all
a.	respect by co-workers	1	2	3	4
b.	my pay	1	2	3	4
c.	opportunity to produce quality work	1	2	3	4
d.	good interpersonal relationships at work	1	2	3	4
e.	chance for promotion	1	2	3	4
f.	fair organization policies	1	2	3	4
g.	opportunity for coming up with new ideas	1	2	3	4
h.	being told that I'm doing a good job	1	2	3	4
i.	freedom to do the job my way	1	2	3	4
j.	opportunity for personal growth and development	1	2	3	4
k.	good supervision	1	2	3	4
l.	good work environment	1	2	3	4
m.	up-to-date equipment with which to work	1	2	3	4
n.	organization benefits	1	2	3	4
o.	feeling that my work is important	1	2	3	4

TABLE 2.6

111. In the left column, check only two which have the highest priority in your organization. In the right column, check only two which have the lowest priority in your organization.

Highest priority (check only two)		Lowest priority (check only two)	
a. _____	customer service and satisfaction	_____	a.
b. _____	profit	_____	b.
c. _____	quality of product/services	_____	c.
d. _____	development of personnel	_____	d.
e. _____	organization image/reputation	_____	e.
f. _____	quality of work life	_____	f.
g. _____	productivity/efficiency	_____	g.
h. _____	product and service leadership/innovativeness	_____	h.
i. _____	research and development	_____	i.
j. _____	long-term organization growth	_____	j.
k. _____	employee safety and health	_____	k.

The audit itself is part of a total organizational development process that can bring participation into the organizational system. In fact, the audit process models the participative process in gathering and analyzing information to make the organization more effective. A major aspect of the audit is feedback with group discussion and assessment of results. Each department has information to use in improving its quality, productivity, and job satisfaction.

Another method of gathering baseline data is through individual and group interviews with managers, supervisors, and employees. Individual interviews are conducted with a representative selection of people from various areas within the organization. Some effort should be made to obtain the different viewpoints and perspectives of the organization. For example, the interviewer might talk with the president and senior managers, as well as opinion leaders from the employee ranks. The interview with each individual should be conducted in a quiet, comfortable, and private setting, such as an office, small conference room, or lounge. Several interviews must be completed to ensure that all viewpoints and departments are represented adequately. In order to evaluate the interviews and make strategic comparisons, the interview questions are usually structured with similar format and content. These interviews may be conducted by inside people or external resources depending on the level of the organization and requirements for confidentiality. An outside resource can be more objective in conducting some interviews.

In some cases, a group interview or focus group is the most efficient way to gather baseline data. The focus group interview involves a group of people who are asked a series of structured questions related to a specific topic or issue. This group is small, perhaps eight to ten people drawn from an employee population, management group, or a particular area or function within the organization. The focus groups that are most compatible are composed of peers rather than people at different levels of the organization. To ensure anonymity, the facilitator should indicate that responses will be reported only in summary form and no individual will be identified in any way.

The focus group interview should begin with some basic information to orient the group and create a rapport between the facilitator and the participants. After this introduction the facilitator usually asks some general questions. In assessing attitudes toward the organization the facilitator might ask, "How would you describe this organization?" The facilitator then requests more specific information related to the topic or issue of concern. Some of these questions may include: "What do you find most rewarding about your work?" or "What do you find most difficult about your work?" Later questions are more specific and focused: "What do you think would make you and your co-workers more productive on the job?" or "In what ways do you think employees could participate in decision making and problem solving to increase efficiency on the job?" At the end of the session, the facilitator may ask if participants would volunteer for an employee problem solving group in their area.

The facilitator will write individual responses on a flip chart to ensure that all statements are charted in the exact words used by the participants. This is important for accurate interpretation later. Focus interviews may also be documented with audio tape recordings if all members agree. However, taping equipment should be as unobtrusive as possible.

The results of this information gathering are summarized and evaluated to create a picture of the organization at that particular time. This is also a primary reference point for charting development factors ranging from attitude change to productivity improvement.

Providing Information and Feedback

All too often the results of survey data and employee questionnaires are put on a shelf or in a file and forgotten. Employees and managers should have some feedback on the results of the information they provided. The format for reporting data may be an executive summary, a computer printout, charts and graphs, anecdotal data, visual models, or numerical tables. Whatever format is chosen, there should be ample opportunity for informal discussion and formal written feedback and analysis of results among management as well as employee groups. Some aspects of this feedback process have been discussed in relation to the Human Resource Audit.

Information is a major linking element in the participative process. Both managers and employees need information and feedback. Employees are expressing an increased interest in knowing more about the business aspects of their organization. Employees also prefer more feedback from supervisors and senior management. More than ten thousand employees participated in a recent survey conducted by the IABC. Employees' current and preferred sources of information within the organization were compared. The results are listed on p. 37.[8]

Current Source of Information

1. Immediate supervisor
2. Grapevine
3. Small group meetings
4. Bulletin boards

5. Employee handbook/booklets
6. General employee publication
7. Local employee publication
8. Annual business report to employees
9. Mass meetings
10. Top executives

11. Orientation program
12. Union
13. Mass media
14. Audiovisual programs
15. Upward communication programs

Preferred Source of Information

1. Immediate supervisor
2. Small group meetings
3. Top executives
4. Annual business report to employees
5. Employee handbook/booklets
6. Orientation program
7. Local employee publication
8. General employee publication

9. Bulletin boards
10. Upward communication programs
11. Mass meetings
12. Audiovisual programs
13. Union
14. Grapevine
15. Mass media

Getting information to all employees through a general orientation is an essential step in implementing the participative process. There should be an organized information campaign using different media, including memorandums, booklets, letters, videotapes, discussions, and special meetings. One article in the company publication or a brief memorandum from the president about a participative philosophy is not enough. An overall theme or message should provide unity for this campaign. For example, a hospital launches a quality campaign called "Making Things Better." An insurance company establishes a development process called "Quality Has Value." A national credit union uses "EQIP," Employee Quality Improvement Program, to build employee skills and esteem. Themes and logos carried through all communication will be a source of identification and reinforce the values of quality improvement.

The choice of communication methods should take into consideration the channels currently used in the organization. A credible and well-read employee publication may be the cornerstone for the information campaign. A popular and visible chief executive may lead the orientation. The immediate supervisor should be a key person in any employee information campaign. The supervisor should have adequate information to communicate with the employees and answer their questions about participation. In addition, the supervisor needs support from the coordinator and planning group. This may mean developing a special information booklet, videotape, or handout material for meetings with employees.

Communication is easier in organizations where there is trust and respect between management and employees. A sudden interest in more open communication or participation may leave some employees skeptical. Consistent and honest communication is a critical element in the working relationship between management and employees in a participative process. Roles related to communication and feedback activities in the start-up process are indicated in Table 2.7.

TABLE 2.7

Individual/ Group	Communication and Feedback Activities
President/CEO	Write letter to all employees Make speech in employee meeting(s) Contribute to article in employee newsletter
Senior Managers	Write letter to functional departments/units Make presentation to employees Present panel discussion Participate on advisory board
Middle Managers and Supervisors	Hold question and answer sessions with employees Meet with senior managers to discuss objectives Report to president on department/unit goals Discuss process informally with employees Call for volunteers from department/unit Train for leader and facilitator roles Lead and/or facilitate groups in department/unit
Internal Director or Program Coordinator	Coordinate people and resources Maintain records and documentation Market the program to management and employees
Employee Opinion Leaders	Gain recognition as employee representatives Meet with senior managers for discussion Have informal conversations with employees Serve as spokesperson at employee meetings
Training Department	Develop or obtain information booklet/handbook Set up training schedule and training program Monitor training effectiveness and training needs
External Resource Person(s)	Meet with president or CEO Interview top executives/managers Plan with internal groups Train initial facilitators and leaders Facilitate analysis and feedback Assist internal coordinator
Facilitator	Complete facilitator training Discuss program with employees Support leader/supervisor Monitor and document group progress Attend facilitator feedback meetings
Employees	Meet with facilitator and/or leader Read information materials Discuss program with supervisor Volunteer for participative groups

With this integrated approach, employees have an opportunity to gather information and feedback from a variety of preferred sources, including immediate supervisors, executives, group meetings, and handbooks. This network of interaction should not stop with the introduction of the first pilot groups. Many of the activities from the senior management level to the employee level can be integrated into a more formal feedback system to support the ongoing operation of the participative process.

The following feedback system is an effective working model based on the formal and informal communication among people who influence and who are involved in group operation. In this model (Figure 2.1), written reports and memorandums are reinforced by regular meetings and informal discussions. These multiple links provide more accurate monitoring, evaluation, and support. Some organizations add other loops to the system, such as facilitator meetings every three weeks, quarterly meetings for all department leaders, and interdepartmental monthly facilitator luncheons. Newsletters are also a part of this communication and feedback system. This feedback network makes implementation easier for management and employees. They can see how the participative process fits into the current organizational structure and hierarchy.

Action Implementation of Pilot Groups

After careful planning and communication, the time is set for action implementation and the start-up of the first pilot groups. Since the working operation of employee problem-solving teams is discussed in detail in Chapter 4, this section will cover only the implementation of the first pilot groups.

There are two basic approaches to kick off the pilot groups: fanfare or quiet beginnings. Fanfare may include a special opening ceremony with a speech from the president and a full-color issue of the company magazine dedicated to quality and productivity. This brings considerable attention to the participative process and to the people involved. They are immediately set up as models to be watched by others in the organization. This approach creates some excitement, but it also puts pressure on the pilot teams and their performance. Expectations are high. However, a team may not succeed in its first project. Members may also experience a false start as they begin working on a problem and require additional training or information. This indicates that the initial training should be more extensive or that the team needs additional support and direction from the leader and facilitator. All of the pilot groups may be successful in varying degrees. If any one team appears to be in trouble or fails to complete its first project, this becomes a visible disaster for the process and for the individual members. The grapevine will tell the story of the groups that failed. This could create a negative environment for other teams and may discourage potential volunteers.

FIGURE 2.1

Information Flow Monitoring and Feedback System

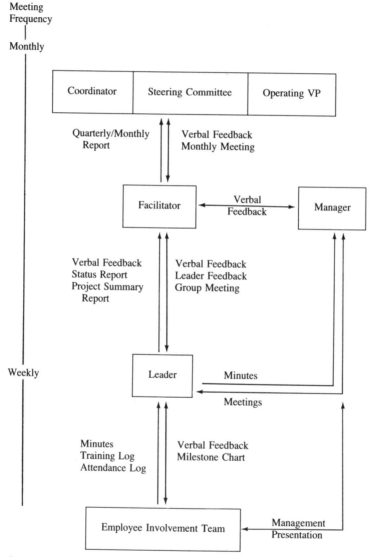

© 1985, B. J. Chakiris Corporation. Reproduced with permission.

Some organizations prefer quiet beginnings as a more appropriate start-up for pilot groups. Several teams begin at the same time and they are monitored carefully by the coordinator. These teams often have contact with each other as they experience the challenges of participation and learn how to work together to solve problems and explore opportunities. These groups are not in the spotlight, but their success is recognized by management and employees with whom they come in contact. The teams work quietly and at their own pace until they are ready for their first presentation to management. Once the initial group projects have been accepted and implemented, the teams may be publicized. For example, the groups may make a presentation at employee meetings or serve as ambassadors by talking to other departments about the participative process. This conservative approach often fits the more traditional organization where management and many employees view the pilot groups as experimental.

Although many organizations view the pilot groups as experimental, the design of the typical participative process is a proven system with tested procedures and training based on experience and application. The only problem may be that some organizations do not recognize or follow this basic system. They may claim that their organization is different with special needs. The most successful participative process is customized for a particular industry or organization, but the concept and basic process are the same for all organizations.

All employee teams essentially follow the same cycle beginning with the training of the leader and facilitator and ending with the completion of the first management presentation and the choice of a new project. In the initial group cycle this process takes approximately six months. The process is illustrated in Figure 2.2. This implementation process is described fully in other chapters of this book.

Evaluating Results

Evaluation focuses on assessing process effectiveness and verifying task results. This documentation helps to explain the benefits of the process to managers and employees. Both quantitative and qualitative data are necessary to evaluate the results of the participative process accurately. Qualitative data may include attitudes of employees and managers, motivational factors, perceptions of productivity, and assessment of organizational strengths and weaknesses. Quantitative data provide information in numerical formats, such as production levels, number of errors or rework, customer complaints, turnover levels, absenteeism, medical costs, and budget figures. Much of the quantitative data is readily available in organizational records and files. The qualitative data on attitudes and practices are more difficult to obtain and require some information gathering and analysis through interviews, audits, and questionnaires. Together the quantitative and qualitative data show changing behavior and attitudes in relation to the participative process.

One simple quantitative measure of success is the level of participation in the employee involvement process. Table 2.8 outlines the participation totals from a

FIGURE 2.2
The Employee Involvement Process

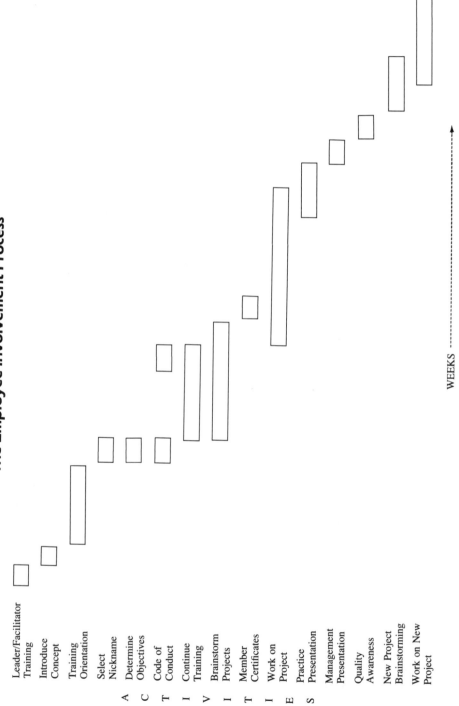

WEEKS --------►

TABLE 2.8

Participation Totals

	No. Teams	No. Potential Volunteers	No. Actual Volunteers	Percentage Volunteers
Division I				
Section A	5	46	41	89.1
Section B	8	84	69	82.1
Section C	21	206	168	81.6
Section D	1	15	14	93.3
Subtotal	35	351	292	83.2
Division II				
Section E	6	72	43	59.7
Section F	10	129	87	67.4
Section G	1	15	8	53.3
Subtotal	17	216	138	63.9
Division III				
Section H	8	109	50	45.9
Section I	16	248	102	41.1
Section J	6	71	48	67.6
Subtotal	30	428	200	46.7

second quarter report. The first quarter was a start-up period with an average participation rate in these divisions of twenty-two percent overall. These second quarter figures show an increase to an over sixty-three percent average participation rate. This is a significant increase reflecting start-up and a positive overall response. However, there are some indications of lower levels of support within specific divisions that may require additional information or coordination.

An average participation rate of over sixty-three percent is substantial. It is unrealistic to assume one hundred percent participation in any process. However, some organizations have been able to gain volunteer rates of eighty percent or more during the first year of operation. This is one quantitative indication of interest and commitment to the participative process.

Another quantitative measure is the result of the first team projects, specifically in the areas of time and cost savings. Time savings is an opportunity for increasing productivity and efficiency. For example, one team saved three hours per day per person by eliminating outdated and unused reports. Another group saved an equivalent amount of employee time by reorganizing its office environment and paper flow. Cost savings are often easier to establish and document. A team in the document processing division of a major organization tackled the problem of poor turnover conditions. The solution was a tray organizer for each sorter terminal and a turnover report. This resulted in a $6,332 cost savings, waste reduction, and overall improvement of the work area. This quantitative information documents the progress and overall result of group work. The formulas and methods for establishing these quantitative measures are described in Chapter 5.

One method of collecting quantitative information for evaluation of attitudes is a questionnaire or survey. If a questionnaire or survey is developed within the organization, it should be pretested to ensure that the instrument is easily understood and that it obtains the information required. Many questionnaires are prepared quickly and often yield little useful information. The survey itself is an intervention or contact with employees and management that can affect employee attitudes. A bad survey instrument can hurt the evaluation process by creating defensiveness or reducing credibility. The coordinator can refer to many reference books for guidance in developing questionnaires and surveys.[9]

The following questions should be thoroughly discussed before developing questions for a management or employee survey:

- Whom do you want to survey?

- What demographic data are needed to interpret responses properly?

- What specific information do you need to obtain?

- What type of format will be most effective in obtaining this information?

- Who will gather the information?

- How will the information be processed and analyzed?

- In what form will results be presented?

The following section was taken from a management survey and focuses on obtaining specific information about attitudes toward quality teams. Managers are asked to respond to the following statements on a scale from strongly agree to strongly disagree. The statements go to the core of management concerns about employee involvement. This information is critical in assessing changes in management attitude and levels of support. The entire survey is included at the end of Chapter 5.

- Quality teams help promote better communication between managers and employees.

- Quality team projects can reduce errors in the work area.

- Quality teams help to increase employee morale.

- Quality teams take too much time away from work activities.

- I feel forced to support quality teams.

- Quality teams lessen my authority over my employees.

- Employees are a good resource for solving problems in the work area.

Interviews and open-ended questionnaires provide a different type of qualitative data. All coordinators enjoy reading statements such as these from leader/supervisor questionnaires and interviews:

"Management support is very good. We were able to go to our manager and discuss problems we were having in our group and he gave us some good points."

"The facilitator is very supportive. He expresses enthusiasm and assists when members are doubtful. He lends security to the group."

"It's becoming like a fever. Everyone is catching it. Nonmembers are finding out that the members are actually getting something out of it . . . and they want it too."

"After our first management presentation there was a lot of pride in the group. It has also brought some of the shy, quiet people out into the open."

The most crucial information for the operation and maintenance of the teams points to specific needs or signals potential difficulty. This allows the coordinator to be proactive rather than waiting until major problems appear. The following statements give the coordinator critical information on underlying feelings and developmental needs:

"While we feel management is supportive of our team, it is also felt that if we didn't have a group, management would not be too concerned."

"Our manager was enthusiastic and asked to sit in on our meetings, but he never followed up."

"Sometimes the facilitator is stronger than the leader and that creates problems."

"The training program is too elementary."

"This particular situation pitted one group of employees against another."

"While we are at group meetings the work piles up and that causes us to get off work an hour late."

"Management lacks tact when reviewing and commenting on the group's presentation. I'm still trying to recover my group."

"Most of our problems are from another area of the division. We can't offer any solutions to the problems we have with that area."

Information and monitoring provide indicators of the following:

■ When additional training with more advanced techniques is needed

■ When teams are struggling and need assistance

■ When teams are successful and deserve recognition

■ The appropriate time frame for further group development within a specific organization

- The integration of the group with departmental structure and procedures

- The relationships among different teams

- The response of top management in dealing with group suggestions and proposals

- Overall management attitude and level of support

- Working relationship between the leader and facilitator

- The specific savings-to-cost ratio in team projects

- Participation rates and project reports

The first year is crucial for any participative process. This is the time for testing, evaluating, and adjusting the program to meet the needs of a particular organization. There will be problems of all sizes, but if the training and the basic operating structure of the process are well defined most problems can be resolved. The communication and feedback system is essential in understanding how the participative process is working within the organization.

The nine-step progression through this chapter—from recognizing the need or opportunity to evaluating results of the first year of operation—establishes a firm foundation and a realistic process for implementing the participative process within the current organizational structure.

References

1. Kanter, Rosabeth Moss. *The Change Masters: Innovation for Productivity in the American Corporation.* New York: Simon and Schuster, 1983.

2. Zander, A. "Resistance to Change: Its Analysis and Prevention." *Advanced Management* 15–16 (Jan. 1962): 9–11.

3. Lippitt, Gordon. *Visualizing Change: Model Building and the Change Process.* Fairfax, VA: National Training Labs/Learning Resources, 1973.

4. Lippitt, Gordon. *Organizational Renewal.* Englewood Cliffs, NJ: Prentice-Hall, 1969.

5. Mink, Oscar G., James M. Shultz, and Barbara P. Mink. *Developing and Managing Open Organizations: A Model and Methods for Maximizing Organizational Potential.* Austin, TX: Learning Concepts, 1979.

6. Deal, Terrence E., and Allan A. Kennedy. *Corporate Cultures: The Rites and Rituals of Corporate Life.* Reading, MA: Addison-Wesley Publishing Co., 1982.

7. "The Human Resource Audit." Metrex Associates, Ltd., 1985. *Facilitation Manual for the Human Resource Audit.* Chicago, IL: B. J. Chakiris Corporation, 1985.

8. Rosenberg, Karn. "What Employees Think of Communication." *Communication World* 2, No. 5 (May 1985): 46–50.

9. The following books are representative of many available resources: Backstrom, Charles H., and Gerald Hursh Cesar. *Survey Research* 2d ed. New York: John Wiley & Sons, 1981: Berdie, Douglas R., and John F. Anderson. *Questionnaires: Design and Use.* Metuchen, NJ: The Scarecrow Press, Inc., 1974; Lavrakas, Paul J. *Telephone Survey Methods: Sampling, Selection, and Supervision* Applied Social Research Methods Series, Volume 7. Sage Publications, Inc. Newbury Park, CA, 1987.

CHAPTER 3
Training for Participation and Employee Involvement

Training is essential in any commitment to the participative process. Most employees cannot be expected to work as a team and effectively identify, analyze, and solve work-related problems without some training and orientation. While these individuals may have enthusiasm and interest, they need specific knowledge of problem-solving techniques, group process, and communication to be effective.

Two primary objectives of the participative process are: (1) to improve efficiency and productivity by increasing quality consciousness and participation in problem solving in the work area, and (2) to improve motivation and morale by developing employee resources and leadership potential, a process that has been called *people-building*. Effective training programs help groups reach objectives, such as increased teamwork, improved communication, creative thinking, quality service attitudes, and more effective manager/employee relationships.

In many organizations, training for participation is a two-step process involving facilitators and group members. The leaders and facilitators attend an intensive training program lasting from three to five days. This group is trained by internal personnel or an outside resource. These leaders and facilitators then go back to their area or department and train the members of their individual teams. Employee training is less formal, although often structured around the same modules and audiovisual materials used in the initial leader and facilitator training. The quality of the employee group training can vary depending on the skill, attitude, and motivation of the individual leaders and facilitators. This two-step training process is beneficial in developing ownership and commitment, and integrating participation into the existing organizational structure. Supervisors who are also team leaders assume more responsibility for the process when they perform a central role in establishing the process in their department or section.

Challenges in the Training Process

There are challenges in any training program, but training for various types of participation is especially critical and will influence the ultimate success of the process directly. While it may be unrealistic to assume that three days of training for leaders and facilitators will provide all the necessary skills, or even a basic understanding of the complex process of group problem solving, some framework must be established. Training for team members extends over the first eight to ten weeks of employee team meetings and may set the tone for the entire group history.

Training for participation and employee involvement may be distinguished from some other types of training because the skills for participation are put into immediate practice. The opportunity for testing skills in the workplace and getting feedback on performance makes this a complete and valuable training cycle. The following guidelines offer a perspective for developing appropriate training for the participative process.

Relate Training Directly to Current Organizational Objectives. Training begins with a strong statement of purpose and a clear grounding in organizational needs, values, and procedures as well as realistic expectations for performance. The focus of participation is specifically on work-related problems that may detract from the efficiency and productivity of a department, area, or function. Teams also consider areas of opportunity that are not necessarily related to problems.

Time spent in training and subsequent workplace meetings represents a substantial corporate investment. Management expects training to pay off in increased productivity and efficiency in relation to specific business goals. While the needs of service industries may be different from those in manufacturing areas and product production, the payoff must be evident. The actual contact with the customer or user becomes an important basis for measuring quality and productivity in service industries. Developing a monitoring and feedback system, reducing error, and establishing effective appraisal and prevention activities often result in substantial cost savings and increased productivity. A well-trained quality team or employee involvement group can provide assistance in these areas with the payoff management expects.

Match Training to the Experience and Developmental Needs of the Group. The experience, attitude, and developmental needs of group members are important to consider. Why are they in the training program? Did their manager recruit them or did they volunteer? Voluntary participation is important. People cannot be forced to participate. Employees must choose participation if the involvement process is to work. Negative attitudes and skepticism in training sessions often are a result of imposed attendance.

Leaders in most employee groups are immediate supervisors. While many leaders have taken basic supervisory training courses, they have not necessarily had training or experience in group interaction and problem solving. Their attitudes toward a participative process such as employee involvement may vary from enthusiasm to quiet hostility.

It is important to stress benefits for everyone in the process. Training benefits leaders and facilitators in their individual development, problem solving skills, and career potential. Employee group members benefit from increased job knowledge, as well as a greater understanding of organizational procedures. The training and subsequent practice of skills is often recognized in the behavior and attitude of individual employees in participative teams. For instance, a manager who initially was not supportive of the employee involvement groups in an organization, admitted seeing substantial positive improvement in the self-confidence and leadership ability of some of the employees in the involvement team. This manager was impressed with the people-building elements of the participative process.

To assess attitudes, needs, and experience of the potential leaders and facilitators, the coordinator and/or training director may want to conduct interviews or surveys before the initial training session. If this is not possible, expectations, concerns, and benefits can be discussed during the first session. The trainer should create enthusiasm and understanding for the participative process by relating individual benefits and integrating them with organizational objectives. Potential leaders and facilitators, as well as the employee teams they will later train, vary in education, experience, job function, and position within the organization. Their background and readiness are not the same. The type of training materials and experiences is a critical factor in the amount of initial involvement and overall learning patterns.

At one time much of the training material produced for various participative teams related to manufacturing and used industrial cases and illustrations. These are not always appropriate for participative training in the service areas where examples and exercises should relate to service problems. While the basic principles of the participative process in service and manufacturing areas are the same, the workbook illustration of marking defects on an engine part may not have any significance to a group of bank tellers. As often as possible, training should be tailored to the particular organization or industry as well as to the individual team members.

Group leaders and facilitators do require some specialized training. In large organizations with many leaders and facilitators it may be possible to have separate training sessions. However, in many organizations leaders and facilitators are trained together. It is important to recognize the differences in the roles of leaders and facilitators, and offer some specialized training for each group of leaders and each group of facilitators around a common core of basic training.

Recognize the Unique Perspective of the Adult Learner. Adult learners have a considerable amount of experience and sophistication. They want to be respected for their knowledge and skill. Most are not anxious for lectures and ironclad rules for success. One of the most common mistakes of inexperienced trainers is in talking down to participants rather than encouraging a level of equality and open communication. The attitude and skills of the trainer determine the effectiveness of the training.

The best format for training adults is one that builds on their present and past experience to improve their current skills and to learn new skills relevant to their present job and to their personal and professional development. Adults are less content to spend time on topics they consider to be unimportant. Training content should be appropriate and relevant to the adult learner. Organization and pacing are also necessary to make the best use of time and resources. Most employees are accustomed to moving around in their work rather than sitting for long periods of time. The training session should have regular breaks and a variety of training activities that allow participants to move about and work in different groups.

Include a Variety of Formats and Opportunities for Team Interaction. Training for participation should model the effective communication and group interaction that will be necessary for the development of employee teams. Group members must be involved early in the session to develop an open communication environment and establish a nonthreatening atmosphere. The trainer should reinforce and encourage all group members to be involved. Group interaction is easier if the training area is comfortable and not too large.

Through direct participation and supportive behavior, members develop enthusiasm for the process. The trainer models the participation process and supportive behavior, helping the group experience the benefits of involvement and teamwork. It should be clear from the beginning that members are expected and encouraged to participate. The trainer must also know the limits of interaction and the necessity for overall progress and movement. Neither the dominant group member nor the quiet member can be ignored.

Training methods should encourage participation and interest. Buzz groups, for example, allow participants to move around and talk in smaller groups. This provides a comfortable forum for members who may hesitate to speak in front of the entire group. Role-playing is helpful for the group in exploring various aspects of a problem or case study. It may also establish a new direction or point of interest. The trainer should debrief and discuss the goals and rationale of each activity and how the outcomes relate to the objectives of the session. This helps the potential leaders and facilitators understand learning objectives and choose appropriate activities for their employee teams.

Using a variety of presentation formats increases interest and group involvement in the learning experience. Visual aids present information more efficiently and highlight key points. Group members should become skilled in using a flip chart. Sheets of paper can be pulled off the pad and taped on walls around the room as a visible record of group effort and progress. Slides, films, and videotapes gain attention and stimulate discussion. For specific information and illustration, overhead projectors are more economical and flexible. Each medium of visual presentation has advantages and disadvantages. An effective presenter chooses the most appropriate medium for the audience and topic.

Developing a Training Program

Whether an organization is considering packaged materials or customized sessions, an outside expert or internal resources, the following questions can help in making strategic decisions about training:

■ What kind of orientation and development does this organization need before beginning the participative process?

■ Who will be trained and what type of training should they have?

- How many people should be trained in the initial sessions?

- Can this training be integrated with current management training?

- Is there commitment for a large-scale expansion in many areas of the organization or only limited expansion in specific areas?

- Is the organization willing to commit a reasonable amount of financial and personnel resources to this process?

- What size budget is available for specialized training and development?

- What are the internal resources of the organization for beginning a participative process and maintaining the process over time?

- Does the training department have films, videotapes, slides, or books relating to participation and employee involvement?

- Are there adequate internal trainers and facilitators available or would new staff have to be hired on a full- or part-time basis?

- Has anyone in the organization previously been involved in the participative process as a leader, facilitator, or trainer?

- What type of external resources will be required?

- Will a train-the-trainer session be required for internal trainers?

- Will the advisory committee need any special training in administering and maintaining the process?

- Will leaders be able to train their departmental team with the assistance of a facilitator or will additional support be needed?

- What skills and knowledge should participants have at the end of the initial training sessions?

- How will this knowledge and skill be evaluated? Will participants take a test or be certified in some manner?

- What type of follow-up and additional training will be needed?

The answers to these questions will assist planning groups in estimating time and personnel costs and in determining the type of training best suited to their needs.

Training for the participative process occurs at several levels over a period of time, and includes general orientation, core training, specialized training, and advanced training. Effective training modules developed especially for the service industry are available in all of these training areas. This chapter will review some aspects of these training modules in problem solving, management presentation, communication, group dynamics, and group leadership.

Framework for Planning a Training Program

Advanced Training	
Special topics	Leaders
	Facilitators
	Employee teams
Specialized Training	
Communication	Leaders
Group dynamics	Facilitators
Group leadership	
Core Training	
Problem solving	Leaders
Management presentations	Facilitators
	Employee teams
General Orientation	
	All members of the organization

Problem-Solving Skills

Core Training

The largest part of core training for the participative process is devoted to problem-solving skills. This is the most popular approach to training for employee team members as well as leaders and facilitators. Typical modules in most programs include the following topic areas:

- Problem recognition
- Brainstorming
- Data collection
- Graphs and charts
- Cause-and-effect analysis
- Process analysis
- Management presentation

A number of modules have been developed specifically for training in the service industry:

- Planning and controlling projects
- Flow charting
- Sampling
- Survey data collection
- Work simplification

■ Work measurement

■ Project benefits and cost analysis

Before using any of these analysis tools it is necessary to understand the problem-solving sequence. This is the unifying element for the entire process. Leaders and facilitators should be equipped to guide the team through this sequence. The result will be a more accurate, appropriate, and realistic solution or proposal based on a logical thought process. One of the reasons for group frustration and failure in problem solving is that groups jump to a solution before the problem is understood or analyzed. A logical procedure or sequence prevents the team from moving ahead before completing the appropriate steps.

In its simplest form the problem-solving sequence includes the following steps: defining the problem, analyzing the problem, developing possible solutions, and choosing the best solution (Table 3.1). Specific driving questions can be used by the leader to move the team through the sequence.

This is a simple, logical sequence with group review and feedback to ensure the best possible team product. This sequence helps the employee teams apply specific problem-solving techniques more effectively. For example, disappointment and dissatisfaction can be eliminated if the team is realistic in its initial choice of a problem. Defining the problem through this analysis can help the members choose a project that they can handle and that will bring them some success. This increases member commitment and confidence. If the team chooses a problem that is too broad, too complex, or beyond its control, the group may not solve the problem even after working for months on the project. Team members need to see some progress and achievement for their efforts. Following the problem-solving sequence can lead the team along a logical and organized path with greater probability for success. Individual problem-solving modules are discussed in detail in Chapter 4.

Through all these techniques, the group generates many possible solutions. The next task is to evaluate this information and make a group decision. The team should develop a list of criteria for evaluation. The following are some techniques for helping the team evaluate alternatives and make a decision.

The Decision Matrix Method. A quantitative answer is established by weighting the criteria in terms of importance and ranking each option in terms of each criterion. The ranking is then multiplied by the weight in each category and totals are established for each option. Figure 3.1 shows a typical decision matrix format. This is used most often when several options or solutions appear to be equally desirable and some comparison or distinction must be made.

The Balance Sheet Approach. This allows the team to evaluate the pros and cons of each option in relation to specific concerns such as effect on the department, reaction from other areas of the organization, or simply the positive and negative consequences (Figure 3.2).

Nominal Technique. This method of evaluation ensures equal contribution from all members based on a total of individual numerical rankings. The nominal method

TABLE 3.1

Facilitative Questions for Problem Solving

Defining the Problem

What are the signs or symptoms to indicate this is a problem?
Is the problem work-related?
How long has the problem existed?
What people or groups does this problem affect?
How serious is this problem?
Can the team solve the problem with available time and resources?
Is the problem clearly defined and limited?
Is the problem within the control of the team?

Analyzing the Problem

What are some possible causes of this problem?
How can the group gather information on this problem?
What are some potential approaches to solving the problem?
How can the team most effectively use time and resources?
What are the most important criteria for the solution?
Is this problem related or linked to other problems?

Developing Possible Solutions

What are some potential solutions for this problem?
Has the group considered a wide variety of possibilities or simply routine options?
Are these solutions creative?
Are these solutions practical for the organization?
Are there other options that the team has not considered?
Does the group need more information in any areas?
Does the list of possible solutions represent the best thinking of the team?
Have all members of the team provided sufficient input to the possible solutions?

Choosing the Best Solution

How can the group narrow the list of possible solutions?
Has the team applied the criteria to each possibility?
Has the team considered the consequences of its choice?
Can the solution be easily implemented?
How can the solution be tested or monitored?
How will this choice affect the organization? people in the department? people in other departments or areas?
Does the team have a contingency plan?
How will the decision be announced or communicated to others?

© 1985, B. J. Chakiris Corporation, *Managing Your Job*. Reproduced with permission.

may be used if there is substantial conflict over the final choices or if the leader wants to be sure that all members have an opportunity to express their preferences. In this approach, team members are given index cards and asked to rank several possible options or ideas. It is important to make sure everyone understands all items before they are ranked. The team should also know the purpose of each round of voting. The cards are collected, shuffled, tallied, and the results are reported. If necessary, voting continues until a clear choice is evident.

Analysis Techniques. No decision should be made without considering the possible consequences of that decision. Techniques such as reverse brainstorming and sce-

FIGURE 3.1

	Criterion A Weighted Value	Criterion B Weighted Value	Criterion C Weighted Value	Total
Option I				
Option II				
Option III				

FIGURE 3.2

Possible Solution: _____	
Advantages	Disadvantages
For our department:	For our department:
For the organization:	For the organization:

nario development are useful in this analysis. Reverse brainstorming is a method for analyzing criticisms of the solutions. In this approach, all possible weaknesses are listed. This is also useful preparation for meeting later objections in management presentations. Scenario development is a more dramatic way of examining consequences. The team develops a plot or sequence of events that might occur if a particular decision were made. Both of these techniques are used after the list of solutions has been narrowed to a few possibilities.

The team should choose the best solution and also have a contingency plan. Working through the group decision process and considering each option in terms of specific problems and benefits can be useful to the team when presenting the proposal to management. The team members will be able to defend their decision and meet possible objections with specific data. Management will know that the team has considered the problem carefully and made a realistic, practical decision on the best solution.

Presentation Skills

Presentation skills are an important part of training for employee teams. They may have an outstanding project, but if the team members cannot communicate their ideas to management effectively in a formal presentation, all their work may accomplish nothing. The management presentation is one of the most critical events for the team. Several key communication skills are required for the group's management presentation:

- Analysis of audience and situation

- Organization of information and visual aids

- Presentation and delivery

- Control of audience questions and challenges

- Evaluation of results and feedback

The management presentation serves the dual purpose of recognizing the team's efforts and presenting recommendations for implementation. A group can also make a presentation to give the status of an ongoing project. However, the best analysis or solution may not be accepted and approved if it is not communicated to management effectively.

The presentation is a visible test of the skills of the team members. In some situations the group is not trained adequately to meet this test of confidence, cooperation, and preparation. Most team members have not had the opportunity to practice making oral presentations. The group members may be excited and enthusiastic about their proposal, but their voices may become soft and monotonous or they may stand stiffly while reading their notes for the management presentation. Careful preparation and presentation training can decrease anxiety and improve chances of management support and approval.

Two important rules apply to the management presentation. The first is *never circumvent the chain of command*. The presentation must be made to the manager to whom the team leader reports. However, if that manager agrees with the team's recommendations but does not have the authority to approve the proposal, the group may make the same presentation to the next higher level of management. The presentation eventually must be made to the manager who has the authority to approve implementation.

The second rule is *no surprises*. One purpose of the participative process is to improve communication. Therefore, the recommendation and progress of a team should be communicated to management through team minutes and verbal discussions before the formal management presentation. However, the oral presentation may be more significant for the team than a written report because there is an opportunity for two-way communication.

Analysis of Audience and Situation

Thinking about an audience of managers and being concerned about management's response to the team and the proposal are sources of anxiety for team members. The team members should begin their planning and practice with a thorough analysis of their audience and the general presentation climate. This helps team members to feel more confident and prepared. The team members should discuss these questions:

- Have all the appropriate people received an invitation to the presentation?

- In what area or "territory" will the presentation be made?

- How much time is available?

- How many people will be present?

- What are their positions within the organization?

- How much knowledge do they have of the project?

- What are their possible attitudes toward the project (positive and negative)?

- Do they have any specific expectations about the presentation?

- Who has the power to make an implementation decision on the project?

Organization of Information and Visual Aids

The team should practice and organize material with this specific audience in mind. The purpose of the presentation is to summarize project activities and make a proposal to management, not to reveal every detail of what the group did over a period of several months. Managers appreciate an efficient use of time during the presentation.

The team members prepare an agenda that lists the sequence of items to be covered and the speakers for each section. This agenda should be sent to all attendees before the meeting. Information for the presentation must be well organized with a logical sequence. First, the introduction catches attention, explains the problem, and sets the pace of the presentation. Only a few major ideas should be included in the actual proposal. The team focuses on the essential elements and provides adequate supporting information for these basic ideas. Finally, the conclusion summarizes major points and suggests appropriate action and implementation.

Charts, graphs, and diagrams are helpful in supporting major ideas. A variety of visual aids increases overall interest and comprehension. In using any type of visual aid the team should ask the following questions about the area in which the presentation will be made:

- What type of room will be used (conference room, office, classroom, auditorium, cafeteria)?

- How large is the room?

- Are there any possible distractions?

- Will there be a podium?

■ How far will the speaker be from the audience?

■ Is a flip chart available? Where should it be placed?

■ How will the charts be mounted on the wall?

■ Can a slide projector or overhead projector be used?

■ Can the room be darkened if necessary?

■ Where are the electrical outlets for equipment?

The team should also keep checklists of all necessary materials and equipment. These include name tags, markers, tape, and extension cords. The group should know how to evaluate the facilities and work most effectively within the space provided.

The team decides what types of visual aids will be most appropriate in making their presentation. The best visual aids are simple and easy to understand. Most teams use charts or graphs written on newsprint or poster board. Many bring in work charts and documentation from team meetings. Members may also show actual items for demonstration and illustration. The leader should discourage the team from becoming too elaborate with audiovisuals. One team might try to outdo the other in the quality or number of visual aids. This is expensive and unnecessary. The following is a list of guidelines for using visual aids:

■ Use simple and relevant visual aids.

■ Do not put too much information on one chart. Make one main point per chart.

■ Use a variety of visual aids to increase attention and interest.

■ Try to give all charts and illustrations some eye appeal. Use color to differentiate items and grab interest. Work with strong, primary colors.

■ Make sure that the letters and figures are large enough for everyone to see without strain.

■ Do not use abbreviations or color codes without making sure that everyone understands what you are doing.

■ Do not use too many charts. This can be boring for the audience. After a while all charts look the same.

■ Make sure that the visual aid is displayed long enough for everyone to see.

■ Use a pointer to call attention to key information.

■ Stand to the side of the visual aid and not in front.

■ Talk to the audience while using the visual aid. Do not turn your back and talk to the visual aid.

Presentation and Delivery

After the team members have completed planning their presentation and the preparation of supporting materials, they begin practicing their delivery and presentation. The members should not just read from a sheet of paper. If the members have been working on a project for months they should know the material. A speaking outline with major ideas and key names and numbers is sufficient in reminding the speaker of essential information. Speaking outlines should be typed on large note cards and key elements highlighted. This allows the speaker to look at the audience and only occasionally glance down at notes.

The team should have at least two dry runs before the actual presentation. If possible, the group can practice the presentation with a video or audio recorder. This allows members to see and/or hear the presentation. Members then evaluate their practice presentation by answering the following questions:

- Are the speakers enthusiastic about the project?

- Do team members seem to know the material?

- Is articulation clear or are the speakers mumbling and slurring words?

- Are the presenters speaking at an appropriate rate, neither too fast nor too slow?

- Is there variety in tone and pace and clear emphasis on key words and figures?

- Is the material interesting?

- Is the progression of ideas logical?

Control of Audience Questions and Challenges

The group should also work together in role playing the question-and-answer session following the presentation. Members might pretend to be managers listening to the presentation, reacting in the way they think management might react and bringing up possible objections. The team spokesperson or moderator fields the questions and answers, both speaking for the group and at times referring specific questions to team members. Everyone should not try to answer every question. Teams may plan that certain members answer questions in particular areas. This makes the process more organized and efficient.

The following practical hints on handling question-and-answer sessions should be considered by groups preparing for their management presentations:

- Repeat the questions to make sure that you understand them and that everyone has heard the question.

- Answer the question as directly as possible without bringing in irrelevant materials.

- Answer only one question at a time. If the question has more than one part, break it up and answer each part separately.

- If you do not know the answer, say so and do not try to fake it.

- Work as a team so that if one member cannot answer the question, another may be able to help.

Evaluation of Results and Feedback

It is essential to start on time, to stay with the agenda, and to think and work as a team during the management presentation. Presentation skills are important to ensure understanding of team ideas and proposals. However, the evaluation of the session will not be based on the ease of presentation or the colorful charts, but on the value and application of the ideas presented. Team members should

FIGURE 3.3

Management Presentation Evaluation

Name _____ Department _____
Project _____ Date _____

Circle the number which best describes how the team accomplished each of these criteria. (1 is the lowest rating and 5 is the highest rating.) If the criteria have not been accomplished write N/A next to the criteria.

	Comments
1. Complexity of the project 1 2 3 4 5	
2. Ingenuity of the solution 1 2 3 4 5	
3. Quality of the presentation 1 2 3 4 5	
4. Impact of productivity within the section 1 2 3 4 5	
5. Savings to the division, department, organization 1 2 3 4 5	
6. Impact of the physical work environment 1 2 3 4 5	
7. Impact on teamwork, attitude between co-workers 1 2 3 4 5	
8. Value in customer servicing 1 2 3 4 5	

© 1985. B. J. Chakiris Corporation. Reproduced with permission.

know the criteria by which their managers will evaluate the proposal. This evaluation form illustrates the significance of business priorities in team projects (Figure 3.3).

Specialized Training

Special components in communication, group dynamics, and leadership are primarily designed for training the leader and the facilitator. Before reviewing these components, it is useful to examine the basic responsibilities of the leader and the facilitator in the participative process.

Facilitator

- Communicates with group, staff, and management
- Maintains appropriate records of team progress
- Executes steering committee or advisory group policy
- Attends group meetings as a resource for group leaders
- Assists the leader in training team members
- Arranges for internal consulting assistance as necessary
- Operates the team temporarily when there is a change in supervisory personnel
- Provides feedback and assistance to the leader in group process and individual development
- Arranges quarterly meetings with management and the group leader to discuss the status of the team

Leader

- Supervises the area or section
- Leads all team activities
- Teaches team members problem-solving techniques
- Provides guidance for group activities
- Ensures proper communication with management and facilitators
- Assures group record maintenance
- Assists in management presentations

There may also be an assistant leader who helps the leader with overall coordination of meetings and documentation. This person may lead the team with the assistance of the facilitator in the absence of the leader.

Communication Skills

Communication is one of the key integrating skills the leader and facilitator use in moving the group through the problem-solving process, creating an effective team with a sense of unity, common goals, and mutual respect. Traditional training programs focus on the quantitative aspects of problem solving. However, the best quantitative training is useless if group members cannot work together and communicate their ideas to management. Leaders and facilitators must have well-developed communication skills. The following sections briefly review some of the communication elements in specialized training, including language, listening, and nonverbal analysis.

Language

Language usage is a practical area in which to start communication training. What words do people use in talking to each other in the group? How does the leader talk to the team? Language that is supportive creates a positive working climate, while negative or evaluative language can cause conflict and defensiveness. The list in Table 3.2 illustrates language approaches that are supportive of the

TABLE 3.2

The Language of Participation

1. *Descriptive language* describes situations and conditions rather than an evaluation or judgment about the situation. The first example describes a situation: "We often have to call customers two and three times before reaching them." The following does not: "These central office people just don't know what they are doing."
2. Language with a *task orientation* focuses on gathering and analyzing information without attempting to control or impose solutions. This type of language might include these statements or questions: "Remember our goals in working with this problem"; "What happens to this application form after it is completed?" These questions help to establish better overall analysis.
3. Language that is *spontaneous* encourages creativity and affiliation. Stiff, formal language can create tension, status differentiation, and defensiveness. Team members should be able to move in some of their own directions with a flexible, adaptable approach to group interaction. The team may establish its own special language patterns including nicknames and "code" terms that have been created out of group experience.
4. Language should reflect *concern and sensitivity* toward other members of the team. The leader may say, "You have worked hard today and we appreciate your effort," or "Do you understand this new procedure or should we talk about it some more?" or "This is a busy time in the department so we will only meet for a half hour today and make the time up after the rush."
5. *"We"* oriented language is more effective than *"I"* language in a group. The leader and facilitator should be especially careful about appearing to be separate or superior to the team. The leader and facilitator should not talk down to the group or emphasize status differences. Equality and unity statements help to bring the team together: "We are all going to help each other tomorrow and give a great management presentation." Analysis and decision making should also be voiced from a "we" perspective: "Do we all agree that this is the best solution?"
6. Language that suggests *flexibility* and *openness* encourages team members to look at all options and approaches. There is always more than one way to consider a problem or opportunity. Language should reflect this open exchange of ideas, "Does anyone have any other suggestions?" The leader can encourage this attitude: "How could we do this differently?" "Are there other causes that we haven't considered?"

team and the task. This language helps to facilitate the problem-solving process and increases understanding and interaction.

The leader and the facilitator can be trained to use language more effectively and support a more positive group climate. Team members should be encouraged to use descriptive language, task-focused language, and unity statements. The leader and facilitator must take responsibility for ensuring comprehension and understanding through effective communication.

Listening

Comprehension involves hearing the words and understanding their meaning. One expert has speculated that only five percent of all communication is understood in the exact manner the sender intended; the rest is based on context and assumption. Poor listening habits are a major reason for misunderstanding and ineffective communication. Many individuals are poor listeners. However, people do listen when they perceive some direct benefit or reward to themselves. The motivation of team members may determine their listening habits. The list in Table 3.3 includes some proven methods for increasing listening skills.

The leader and the facilitator should also be aware of the following techniques to improve the comprehension and listening of team members during group discussion at regular meetings:

■ Follow a logical pattern of thinking. Do not jump from one idea to another.

■ Use verbal transitions to connect ideas.

■ Illustrate ideas with examples, especially those with which the members can identify.

■ Repeat important content items.

■ Speak slowly but maintain variety in tone.

■ Speak with energy and enthusiasm.

■ Stress key words with voice emphasis.

■ Do not mumble or look down while speaking.

These suggestions are based on the delivery as well as the organization of ideas. The leader is in a strategic position to model both effective listening and speaking for the team members. The group will use good communication habits if these skills are taught and reinforced in team interaction throughout the process of participation.

Nonverbal Analysis

While listening to someone speak, people often make many specific evaluations based on nonverbal clues and impressions. These judgments may include personality, competence, and commitment, as well as intelligence and socioeconomic back-

TABLE 3.3

Improving Your Listening Skills
A Guide for Team Leaders and Members

1. *Do not fake attention.* This is essentially non-hearing. Yet listeners seek to make the speaker believe that they are listening. Techniques include repeating key phrases such as "right," "I see," "uh-huh," and other pseudo feedback. In face-to-face contact, the listener may appear to be looking at the speaker intently, leaning forward and nodding the head, yet not hearing anything. Do not let yourself get into the habit of faking attention. Force yourself to ask questions and become actively involved in listening.
2. *Concentrate on listening.* If you are worried about something else, distracted by outside noises, or daydreaming it may be difficult to concentrate on a particular discussion. Listening takes a substantial amount of energy and focused attention. Try to focus on the speaker and what this person is saying. Notice the facial expression and stress on particular words. Reduce physical distraction and competing noises if possible. Listening takes some effort, but it is an important responsibility as part of the team.
3. *Do not make premature evaluation of the speaker or topic.* Often, the speaker's pitch, use of words, accent, or mannerisms might cause you to make a negative judgment and discount *anything* the person may say. Or, you may have no specific interest in the topic and therefore dismiss the speaker's ideas and information. This is not fair to you or to the speaker. You can always learn something new by listening. Recognize your bias and keep an open mind in all discussion and analysis.
4. *Reduce your emotional reactions.* Specific words may cause strong emotional responses in some listeners. These reactions are often intense and may be either positive or negative. It is important to know your own "god terms" and "devil terms" so that you can avoid the reflex responses that they often bring. If you moderate strong emotional reactions you can listen more effectively and increase overall comprehension. This is important in reducing conflict and misunderstanding.
5. *Avoid personal identification and defensiveness.* Sometimes listening is difficult if the listener takes everything personally and responds in a defensive fashion. Some individuals act in this way without realizing it. Others carefully calculate their answer to the assumed attack. They may not listen because they are planning an answer or stewing in anger over the previous statement. Try to be objective and logical in your listening.
6. *Focus on major ideas rather than getting caught up in details.* When listening to a complex or technical subject, it is easy to get involved in taking detailed notes and trying to remember everything rather than listening for the major ideas. It may be helpful to make a mental outline of the most important ideas. Look at the speaker and try to understand what is being said.

ground. While there may be other kinds of evidence to support these assessments, nonverbal clues in appearance, manner, facial expression, posture, movement, voice quality, and pattern are often used to determine meaning. These nonverbal elements may support, modify, or even contradict verbal behavior. Most experts agree that the majority of meaning in communication is in nonverbal dimensions. For example, an employee may say, "I enjoy my work here." Yet the lack of energy and enthusiasm in his voice, the slight sagging of his shoulders, and the lack of direct eye contact may indicate the opposite. While most people can choose appropriate words to disguise their feelings it is more difficult to hide the nonverbal clues. Therefore, the nonverbal elements of communication are prime indicators of the value and intensity of communication interaction.

The leader and facilitator should be aware of nonverbal messages both from individuals and from the team as a whole. This means sensing the frustration, the unity, the potential conflict, the friendship, and the needs of the team even if these are not evident in the language. Words are only a part of the total communication process. Nonverbal elements may include the following:

■ Body movement, facial expression and gesture

■ Vocal characteristics and delivery

■ Space relationships and interpersonal distance

■ Time orientation

■ Display and use of objects and artifacts

All of these nonverbal dimensions affect communication whether the individual is aware of them or not. A selection of nonverbal analysis exercises is shown in Table 3.4. In training sessions, potential leaders and facilitators analyze these

TABLE 3.4

Situation I

The team leader always comes in just as the meeting is scheduled to begin and spreads folders and other materials across one end of the table. Team members leave two chairs on either side of that end of the table and no one ever sits there. This allows the leader approximately one-third of the table space while the group sits around the other two-thirds of the table. The team always waits for the leader to express his ideas before anyone speaks. The leader often begins with a ten-minute review of progress.

■ What is the relationship of the leader to this team?

■ Why might group members be hesitant to participate?

■ What would you do to encourage more openness and spontaneity in this group?

Situation II

Two good friends, Molly and Sandra, come into the team meetings together, talking and laughing. They always sit next to each other. Both Molly and Sandra are enthusiastic and active group members. Suddenly they are not sitting together. During the last two meetings they have not spoken directly to each other. Their level of energy and involvement in the group is low. The other team members are uncomfortable and do not know what to do.

■ What could be causing the changed behavior of Molly and Sandra?

■ How do their actions affect the rest of the team?

■ As leader or facilitator, what would you do about this situation?

Situation III

Dan tends to come into the team meeting and sit in the far corner. He often moves his chair a foot or so away from the table and leans back slightly in his chair. His body is generally oriented away from the people even when he is talking to the group. Most team members just ignore Dan.

■ What do you think is Dan's attitude or feeling toward the group?

■ Why does the team ignore Dan?

■ What could you do to make Dan more a part of the group?

situations in terms of the nonverbal information and determine appropriate responses in relation to the people and the situation.

Group Dynamics Skills

The leader and facilitator must understand group dynamics and be aware of individual needs as well as overall team development. This means being able to recognize verbal and nonverbal cues that signal the need for information, structure, emotional support, tension release, or focus.

Problem-solving groups can be a powerful asset for the organization. In many cases teams do make better decisions than individuals because of the increased amount of information, more effective division of labor, error correction, and evaluation. Teams also tend to be more creative by using group energy and cumulative ideas. Even when decisions must be made by an individual such as the CEO, management groups serve as resources and provide valuable input.

The power of employee teams in a participative process comes from the diverse personalities and a wide range of knowledge, yet these same factors can also bring conflict to the group. While disagreement over issues and ideas may bring a more effective final decision, the conflict of personalities can be difficult to resolve. Team members bring many individual attitudes, experiences, and needs into the group. It is often a real challenge for these diverse people to work together unless there is a common commitment to the team and group goals. Often the only initial commonality that members have is working in the same department or area or having similar jobs within the organization. There may be a number of hidden agendas or individual motives among group members, but individuals will remain in the group and support the team as long as they believe they can meet some of their individual goals. The recognition that the team receives may also be an incentive for some members.

As noted in Chapter 1, individuals have different needs for belonging to groups. For some, the group is a major source of recognition and inclusion. Others are not as dependent on identity and association with their organization or co-workers. Individuals also vary in the amount of control and influence they need within a group. Some are most comfortable serving in a leadership role, while others are content to be followers and need only direction and structure. Individuals may express these needs in varying intensity. The involvement team must satisfy some of these individual needs to maintain group energy and effectiveness.

Group Process

Groups go through stages of development that may include orientation, conflict, cohesion, and accomplishment. Diverse individuals develop and learn through a process that brings them together as a working team. The initial stage of group development is often a period of orientation and testing of process and relationships.

Some of the team members may be uneasy or uncertain about what will happen in the group and how they will work together. This is a time when there should be a clear identification of tasks and procedures. In quality circles and other participative groups the team often creates a code of conduct as one of their first group activities. This sets many of the basic norms of group behavior and interaction.

A code of conduct can prevent future difficulties by establishing a system of mutual respect for the team's own version of "law and order." The following code of conduct was developed by a typical employee involvement group:

Be on time

Be prepared

Bring pencil, paper, and other needed items to meetings

Be responsible for your duties

Participate fully

Pay attention

Majority rules

Majority present for voting

Unexcused absences will be evaluated by team

Do not interrupt

Do not criticize others

Listen to all ideas

Be open for suggestions

Respect confidentiality

Be courteous

Respect other members' feelings

Everyone is equal

Don't lose your temper

Be cooperative

Be fair

Have fun

Help with setup and cleanup

Explain to other members if you decide to drop out

No smoking

After orientation, the team should begin to discuss issues and ideas more openly. However, the initial tension may be replaced by some personality conflicts and differences of opinion. This stage of group development provides an opportunity for the team to enforce its code of conduct in resolving disputes and maintaining courtesy and mutual respect. There may be some disagreement, as members feel more comfortable expressing their ideas. Some might question the task and direction of the group. The members may spend a great deal of time in active discussion with little resolution.

This is a critical stage for team morale and motivation. Members can be frustrated if the group does not seem to be making any progress. At this point the leader and facilitator help focus the team and encourage active consideration of possible projects. With appropriate guidance from the leader and facilitator the group moves through this stage to a point where there are established roles and responsibilities. Through all the discussion and disagreement the team begins to integrate. The members start to gather information for the first group project. There is a growing group cohesiveness and team feeling. Members still disagree, but there is respect for all opinions. Everyone in the team has some conformity to group norms. There is a common goal with open communication and cooperation. The group is now ready to work together as a real team.

Group Roles

In the beginning of team development, few roles are clear. Members and the leader and facilitator try to find their appropriate behavior or position in the group. Many members are more quiet and restrained than usual. Everyone is overly polite. Soon there are certain expectations or predictions of behavior from a particular member. For example, "Tom always makes us laugh," or "Jan asks good questions to make us think about the situation." However, individuals may be caught in particular roles when they would rather not be stereotyped as "the clever one" or "the loudmouth." A healthy team allows members to be flexible in their roles. This flexibility may be enhanced by rotating duties and responsibilities.

The leader and facilitator should recognize specific roles and how these roles affect the team as a whole. Task roles and people roles are especially helpful in overall group maintenance. However, some individual roles may hurt the teamwork and unity, distract group goals, and interrupt team progress and development. The list in Table 3.5 describes some of the most common task roles, people roles, and individual roles within the group.

Team Development

One of the responsibilities of the leader and facilitator is to document team progress and development in regular reports to management, the advisory board, and the program coordinator. A list of criteria to measure team progress is shown in Table 3.6.

TABLE 3.5

Task orientation roles	Initiator
	Information seeker
	Elaborator
	Summarizer
	Disagreer
	Pacer
	Agreement checker
People orientation roles	Encourager
	Harmonizer
	Compromiser
	Gatekeeper
	Tension reliever
	Supporter
Individual orientation roles	Blocker
	Aggressor
	Dominator
	Clown
	Manipulator
	Sleeper

Team Building

One of the key elements of group development is effective team building. The leader and facilitator should encourage and model effective team building techniques. Team building can also be developed as the group recognizes its accomplishments and creates a group history and identity based on shared experiences.

The team should agree on major objectives and goals. These guidelines are written and distributed to all group members. The leader should remind members of these objectives as they choose projects and begin to work together. The team learns to recognize progress in work the members have done together. Setting smaller goals in relation to the larger objectives and noting milestones along the way are important to group morale. As the group takes time to celebrate success and accomplishment as a team, a group spirit is developed. This means compliments for the group including, "We did a great job on this project," and rewards such as taking time to socialize together.

Team members are encouraged to use unity terms such as "we" and "our." This places the verbal and psychological emphasis on the group as a whole. The team that takes time to integrate new members into the group and talk about the loss of other members is a stronger, more integrated unit. The group must also deal with bringing someone back onto the team who may have dropped out for a time. Careful and caring entry and exit procedures make the members aware of their unity and interrelatedness.

The team may also have its own special name that gives it an identity and represents the members' goals and values. *The Perfect Circle, Proud Producers,* and *The Intellectuals* reflect team members' feelings about themselves and their

TABLE 3.6

Understanding of Work Unit
Can members describe the business of their work unit?
Do they know the general work flow?
Are they aware of interaction with other areas and departments?

Insight of Work Issues and Complexity
Does the team assess the impact of proposed changes on people concerned?
Do they understand the impact on productivity and costs?

Organization
Are minutes taken of the meetings?
Does the team gather and use the resources they need?
Is past progress summarized and new action reported?
Does the team plan effectively?

Procedures and Norms
Is the team run according to the code of conduct?
Does the code need revision?
Are procedures flexible?
Are procedures appropriate to the group?

Communication
Do members feel comfortable speaking to the group?
Does the team use *we* words?
Do members express their ideas clearly and concisely?
Does the team communicate through timely minutes and reports?
Does the group maintain contact with management and other teams?

Participation
Are members enthusiastic about attendance?
Does everyone participate in the process?
Do members volunteer for group work?
Is the team making full use of group resources, skills, and knowledge?

Cooperation
Do team members help each other?
Is work responsibility spread equally?
Do group members actively support each other?
Are members open-minded and willing to listen to other ideas?
Do team members seem to like each other as friends and colleagues?

Loyalty, Identity, and Morale
Are members motivated?
Are members eager and enthusiastic about projects?
Is there a sense of cohesiveness in the group?
Do members care about the group and about each other?
Do members seem to enjoy the problem-solving process?
Can the team accept failure without feeling defeated?

Response to Leadership
Is the group open to the leader's suggestions?
Can the leader influence the group?
Does the team respect the leader?

Group Confidence and Initiative
Are members taking the initiative for task work and procedures?
Do team members take responsibility for organizing?
Do members keep the communication going without intervention of the leader?
Does the group feel confident and competent in their task?
Do team members seem satisfied with the group decision?

TABLE 3.6 (Continued)

Conflict Resolution
Does the group recognize and resolve conflict?
Do the members focus on issues rather than personalities?
Can the group reach a compromise?
Does the team use consensus?
Does the team gather adequate information to understand disputed issues?

Acceptance of Differences
Do people listen to each other?
Can differing opinions be expressed openly?
Do members gather information on all sides of an issue?
Can the team accept criticism?

task. The team name is often displayed on a banner or poster during group meetings. Some groups also wear buttons with their team name or slogan. This name, slogan, or logo may also be used in reports, presentation materials, and in departmental newsletters. Choosing a name is often one of the first tasks of the group and the initial unifying force.

Teams should be encouraged to develop their own rituals and ceremonies, such as welcoming a new member to the group or celebrating the birthday of a team member. This is one method by which the group creates its own history based on shared experiences. Teams often recall their history with statements such as: "Remember our first management presentation? We were so nervous. Mary and Ed couldn't get the chart to stay on the board." Stories of success and failure help to bring the team together. The members are all a part of those experiences. It is especially important to recall how group members supported or helped each other through good and bad times. The team may also have some fantasies of "super group" accomplishment or imaginary adventures together. Members may have special terms or phrases that refer to their group history, experience, or fantasy. All of these actions make the group bond stronger.

The team must also see examples of unity and cooperation in the behavior of its leader and facilitator. The team should know that this support system is solid and consistent. If the leader and facilitator have a personality clash or disagreement, this should not be evident in front of the team. If differences cannot be resolved easily, the facilitator may ask for reassignment. The leader and facilitator are models for teamwork and unity. This means mutual respect and cooperation toward promoting team development.

Case studies are useful in understanding specific group situations that can cause problems in motivation, morale, and task orientation. The leader and facilitator apply their knowledge of group process and roles to analyze the situation and suggest possible actions for improvement. For example, the following case study on individual roles is based on an actual group experience.

TEAMWORK

The checklist in Table 3.7 can be used in the participative process to evaluate team development.

TABLE 3.7

Checklist of Team Development

Team Name _____ Department _____
Date _____

	Excellent	Good	Average	Below Average
Understanding of Work Unit				
Insight of Work Issues and Complexity				
Organization				
Procedures and Norms				
Communication				
Participation				
Cooperation				
Loyalty, Identity, and Morale				
Response to Leadership				
Group Confidence and Initiative				
Conflict Resolution				
Acceptance of Differences				
Overall Development				

Comments:

Case Study

Wanda always arrived at team meetings late, wearing sunglasses and looking bored. She often ate during the meeting. The other team members tried to ignore her and her noisy chewing. Wanda never said anything to anyone in the group. Group progress slowed down since Wanda joined the team approximately two months before. Members spent a lot of time outside the meeting complaining about her. There was an obvious decline in group morale and energy.

After the most recent meeting, the facilitator and the leader met to discuss Wanda. The supervisor-leader recounted a long list of previous difficulties with her: tardiness, errors, bad attitude, and messy workspace. The supervisor did not see anything positive or hopeful in Wanda's behavior. "I try to get her motivated, but she just doesn't seem to care about anything. She just does enough to get by." He was prepared to recommend that Wanda not be included in future team activities. "I don't know why she even comes to meetings, but she is always there," he said.

What do you think Wanda's appearance and behavior mean?

What do you think is her motivation for acting this way?

If you were responsible for this team what would you do?

How could you as leader or facilitator integrate Wanda into the team?

What could the team do to help integrate her into the group activity?

This situation was finally resolved by the facilitator and the leader. They were determined to understand Wanda and help her. At the next meeting the facilitator noticed that there were times during an especially spirited discussion when Wanda seemed to tilt her head as if she wanted to say something. When Wanda tilted her head again the facilitator intervened and asked her opinion. To everyone's surprise, Wanda spoke and made an intelligent, useful suggestion. The facilitator spoke to the team leader and he agreed to offer his support by giving Wanda some recognition and bringing her into the discussion, especially when he saw her tilt her head.

After a few more meetings Wanda became a productive part of the team. She stopped wearing sunglasses and arrived at every meeting on time. She no longer ate during the meetings. However, one day she brought apples for everyone from a tree in her backyard. The supervisor was pleasantly surprised with the improvement in Wanda's work attitude. He gave her increased departmental responsibility and noted improved efficiency and motivation in her annual performance review. The group also responded to Wanda's contributions and began to include her in the departmental "lunch crowd." Wanda is a part of the team because a facilitator and leader took time to recognize her and her potential contribution to the team. This resource could have been lost without the insight and intervention of a well-trained facilitator and a flexible leader.

Team Leadership Skills

Group leaders are often classified according to the amount of control they exert on the members, ranging from the absolute power of the authoritarian leader to the abdication of the *laissez faire* leader. Somewhere in between is the true test of leadership. The team leader in the employee involvement process provides structure and support and yet allows people to grow and develop as individuals and as team members. This leadership style is a balance of task and people orientation. The group leader's responsibilities include managing process and managing people.

Specific leadership skills can be taught, and many of them may already be a part of the behavior of effective supervisors and managers. Employees recognize and appreciate good leadership. The qualities most often associated with effective leadership and supervision are competence and job knowledge, maturity and emotional stability, honesty and fairness, and friendliness and accessibility. The leader with these qualities provides support and security for the team.

The leader trains the team and later guides the group through the actual problem-solving process. In the beginning of team development, it is essential that the group have a strong effective leader. Later, as the team matures and develops its own strengths and skills, the leader may take a less directive role. The leader should eventually delegate many responsibilities to members to begin their leadership development. An assistant leader and/or a rotating leader may also be used with a more experienced team.

Managing Process

Both the team leader and the facilitator have leadership functions. In managing all these elements they learn to work on two levels, analysis and action. The analysis level comes first and continues throughout the team interaction. As soon as the group comes into the room the leader must begin analyzing the situation. What is the general attitude of the group? Are the members ready to begin working immediately or do they need a few minutes of informal talk before starting? Is the team prepared? During the discussion the leader should continue analysis. Do the team members understand? Are they all working from the same perspective? Are there ideas that are not being expressed but are strongly evident? Are good ideas being passed over too quickly? Does the team need direction? Information is gathered and processed in the mind of an effective leader assessing the needs and the status of the team in relation to specific goals.

Observation and analysis often point to direct action on the part of the team leader. For example, the leader may take action to mediate or diffuse potential conflict. This action may take the form of a simple statement or a direct question. The group leader may recognize a need to focus the attention of the team in specific areas rather than wander from one direction to another. A summary statement or a question to check on agreement may be critical in maintaining team morale and task orientation.

Sometimes the leader delays any direct action, waiting for the team to recognize the need and refocus its efforts or allowing the members to resolve a disagreement among themselves. This permits the members to develop their own leadership skills in managing group task activities. Team members should also learn to summarize, focus, check agreement, and link ideas. This is the responsibility of all members and an indicator of effective team communication and development.

Group leaders sometimes do not see overall team movement. They may focus on more specific actions or individuals rather than general elements of group development. The effective team leader recognizes the direction, pace, and the quality of group work as well as the connection each individual is making in relation to the total team effort. This communication management model (Figure 3.4) is useful in teaching the leader as well as the team members to sense the overall communication flow of the group and helps the team coordinate its efforts toward a specific goal. It provides the leader with structure and process in order to apply analysis to group activities, decisions, and actions. This process begins with orientation and ends with making closure, but the bulk of team activity is in the dynamic cycle which moves among the internal elements: focusing attention, recognizing progress, getting agreement, summarizing, and linking. These communication elements are cyclical in nature rather than sequential. The flow is determined by the needs of the team at any particular time.

Table 3.8 lists the leadership responsibilities in the communication management model.

Managing People

The team leader plays a number of important roles in relation to the employee group. The facilitator may also be involved in these roles in supporting the team leader. These leadership roles fall into the following categories:

Leader as Manager

- Planning

- Assessing available resources

- Assigning responsibility

- Maintaining documentation

- Establishing structure

- Evaluating process

Leader as Trainer and Educator

- Presenting information clearly

- Using illustrations and examples

- Asking effective questions

- Checking for comprehension and application

Leader as Motivator

- Getting people involved

- Maintaining commitment

- Providing support

- Showing enthusiasm

FIGURE 3.4

COMMUNICATION MANAGEMENT CYCLE

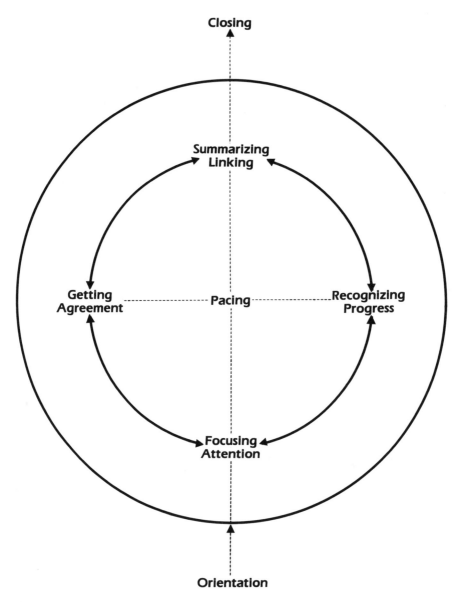

© 1985, B. J. Chakiris Corporation. Reproduced with permission.

TABLE 3.8

Orientation

Opening meetings with agenda and goals
Giving pertinent data to orient the team
Bringing the team up-to-date
Preparing team for work

Focusing Attention

Keeping on the topic
Not getting off track with irrelevant material
Reducing unnecessary or repetitious discussion
Limiting discussion to essential elements
Maintaining direction and focus

Summarizing/Linking

Rephrasing ideas
Clarifying
Checking accuracy
Unifying major ideas
Establishing transitions

Recognizing Progress

Citing progress toward goals
Recognizing accomplishment
Acknowledging progression
Stating "where we are now"

Getting Agreement

Establishing common ground
Making a statement of consensus
Providing support for cooperation
Checking for agreement
Clarifying points of agreement

Pacing

Recognizing amount of time spent in each area
Being aware of the amount of time remaining
Reporting to group on time elements
Setting priorities for time usage
Refusing to spend too much time in one area
Accomplishing objective in efficient time span

Closing

Establishing progress during meeting
Reviewing key information
Establishing responsibilities for action
Preparing for next meeting

TEAMWORK

- Recognizing success
- Rewarding accomplishment

In these basic roles the leader or facilitator can help manage team direction. The model (Figure 3.5) is useful in recognizing where the team is and what the essential needs are at any particular time in group development. The balance is between task and people needs. While the group may work on either end of the

FIGURE 3.5

COMMUNICATION BEHAVIOR MODEL

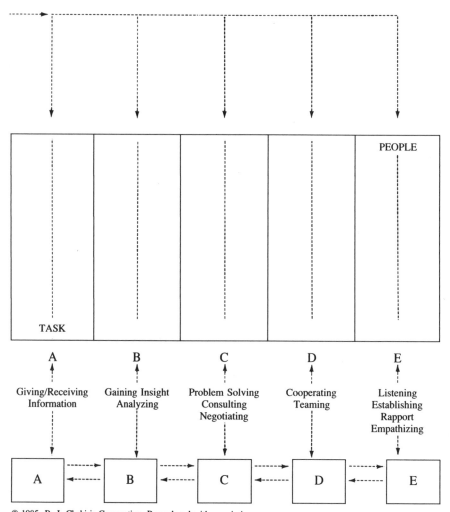

scale requiring more task support or people support at different times, the group works best with a balance of task and people orientation. This is the point at which the team is a unified, problem-solving force.

This model helps the leader visualize group communication along a task-people continuum from information exchange to interpersonal support. Team needs are not constant, so there are different requirements for task orientation and people orientation in various situations.

Each team has its own distinct personality. Most groups perform their jobs well and have a collection of awards including paperweights, pins, and letter openers that they received as rewards for their service to the organization. These teams are representative of the majority of employee involvement groups. However, other teams seem to get more attention, both positive and negative. These are the teams that are a challenge for the leader, facilitator, and coordinator. The problem with many of these difficult groups is that they get stuck in particular patterns that cause them to become ineffective in their task behavior or inappropriate in their social behavior.

Table 3.9 includes descriptions of teams that may provide some challenges for the leader and the facilitator. Each of these groups has been given a dominant "personality" name to demonstrate particular characteristics. These names should not be confused with the names teams give themselves. These descriptions and situations provide exercises for leader and facilitator training to encourage discussion and analysis of group patterns. A worksheet (Figure 3.6) is provided for these exercises.

The leader and facilitator should recognize these emerging group patterns before the group behavior and norms are firmly established. Teams create their roles and expectations early in group development. These norms are more difficult to modify or change later. Leaders and facilitators should be especially aware of balancing task and people orientation within the group. Potential dysfunctional group personalities may begin with: (1) dominant individual roles, (2) lack of appropriate structure and procedure initially, or (3) inadequate or inappropriate training.

A study of group personalities can be helpful to the leader and facilitator in recognizing major group traits and helping team members to use their skills and resources in a positive manner to reach group goals. A variety of case studies and role-playing situations help team leaders practice their skills on the level of analysis and action. It may also be useful to have potential leaders and facilitators talk about their overall perceptions and concerns in relation to their role. Leaders and facilitators should develop a rapport or understanding that can serve as a support system as they move into their team leadership roles.

Evaluation and Follow-up for Training

After the initial training is completed there should be some method of evaluation. Are these potential leaders and facilitators prepared to go back and train their

TABLE 3.9

Group Profiles

Stars

This group is made up of resourceful high achievers. Members have a great deal of enthusiasm and task orientation. They are loyal to the organization and its goals. This group is motivated by status, power, and recognition. They need some amount of influence and control, but give back hard work and significant accomplishment in reaching organizational goals. There are those within the organization who may be jealous and resentful of the Stars especially when management identifies them as the ideal group.

Firecrackers

This group is vocal and often aggressive in its approach. Members have a substantial amount of energy and enthusiasm for their task. The Firecrackers are willing to challenge authority in their zeal for their projects. They are motivated by action and influence. The Firecrackers want to get something done quickly to change or improve the organization. Their energy may be short-lived with some erratic stops and starts.

The Sleepers

This group is passive and reserved. They do not create any problems or conflicts. Whenever they have a group meeting, members often just sit and stare at each other. Everyone comes to the meetings, but nothing gets done. There is a general lack of initiative and energy. The Sleepers are not motivated or enthusiastic about anything.

Party Animals

This group is highly social with many individual roles. They have great energy, but it is most often misdirected into social activity with no obvious task orientation. Members enjoy social contact and getting away from their desk for an hour. Their major goal is to have fun. They are likeable and outgoing people. They bring refreshments to their meetings and sometimes they play music to create a nicer atmosphere. The Party Animals have many excuses for not getting the work done.

Plodders

This group is extremely task oriented. They believe in careful analysis and attention to detail. They may get lost in the process and never move to action. Simple projects take them a long time. These analytical people want to do a thorough job. They have to be sure there are no mistakes in their figures so they check and double check. The Plodders do provide good information and accomplish most tasks on time. However they are seldom recognized.

Crusaders

This group is also task oriented, but with a mission to convert the organization to a more efficient operation. They are enthusiastic and highly motivated. Sometimes they are overzealous in their efforts and alienate some employees. They may monitor work activities, constantly looking for inefficiency. They enjoy the challenge and the cause that requires work and dedication. They believe in quality and efficiency and they want everyone else to believe as well.

---

teams? Do they know the rules for brainstorming, how to make a Pareto chart, or methods for improving management presentations? Can they handle group conflict or dominant individual roles? The leader and facilitator should know how to apply this knowledge and skill in employee teams.

Training evaluation is handled in several different ways. Some organizations give a formal final examination and certify members for successful completion of the training. Other organizations merely certify the leaders and facilitators after they attend all the training sessions. In some instances, participants take home a

FIGURE 3.6

Leadership Analysis and Action Worksheet

Directions: Choose one of the group descriptions and put yourself in the role of the new leader or facilitator of that particular group. After some individual analysis in completing the worksheet, meet in groups to discuss action steps and analysis.

Team Name: _____

What are the most dominant characteristics of this group?

What are their major strengths? | weaknesses?

What impact do they have or potentially have on organizational goals?

If you were in a leadership position in this team what would you do to improve the group?

Task Level | People Level

final evaluation that they complete and then meet with the trainer for an individual discussion and analysis. Some training sessions also include a regular quiz or assessment as part of the session. Whatever method is chosen, some evaluation is essential to the success of the total process. Leaders and facilitators also tend to take the training activities more seriously if they know they are responsible for learning the material.

Some organizations offer additional formal training after twelve to eighteen months. This may be a review of previous material or information on new techniques. Advanced training and periodic meetings of leaders and facilitators to discuss common problems are important to maintain momentum in any involvement process. Leaders and members appreciate learning new techniques, ideas, and approaches. After the first year of the program, they may have solved the most obvious problems and want to tackle more difficult ones. An advanced training session inspires a leader and provides assistance for more complex team projects. Additional techniques for increasing creativity, gathering and analyzing information, or improving management presentations are usually well received by the team.

Project updates, newsletters, and information bulletins from the training division may also continue the learning process for leaders and build a valuable resource network for the entire team. Many work units also have their own newsletter reporting on the activities of employee involvement groups with information on the latest team projects and pictures of group members in action. This method of communication records group progress and shares accomplishments.

The real test of training is the effectiveness of the team in solving problems and improving efficiency and productivity in the department. Training in problem-solving skills provides information and skills employees can use every day in their workplace. Presentation skills are valuable as individual employees learn to express their ideas in an organized and persuasive manner. Communication and group dynamics help create a more open sharing of information and cooperation among employees and supervisors. Leadership training can increase the supervisor's skills in managing people and resources. Training is one of the most significant activities available to an organization to ensure success in the participative process.

Resources

Problem Solving

deBono, Edward. *Lateral Thinking: Creativity Step by Step.* New York: Harper & Row, 1970.

Delbecq, Andre L., Andrew H. Van de Ven, and David Gustafson. *Group Techniques for Program Planning: A Guide to Nominal Group and Delphi Processes.* Glenview, IL: Scott, Foresman, 1975.

Fisher, B. Aubrey. *Small Group Decision Making* 2d ed. New York: McGraw-Hill Book Co., 1980.

Gouran, D. *Making Decisions in Groups: Choices and Consequences.* Glenview, IL: Scott, Foresman, 1982.

Hare, A. P. *Handbook of Small Group Research* 2d ed. New York: The Free Press, 1976.

Maier, N. R. F. *Problem Solving and Discussions, and Conferences.* New York: McGraw Hill, 1963.

———. "Assets and Liabilities in Group Problem Solving: The Need for an Integrative Function." *Psychological Review* 74, (1967):239–49.

Osborn, Alex F. *Applied Imagination: Principles and Procedures of Creative Problem Solving* 3d ed. New York: Charles Scribner's Sons, 1962.

Prince, George M., *The Practice of Creativity: A Manual for Dynamic Group Problem Solving.* New York: Harper & Row, 1970.

Wright, G. *Behavioral Decision Theory: An Introduction.* Beverly Hills, CA: Sage, 1984.

Presentation

Andrews, J. R. *Public Speaking: Principles into Practice.* New York: Macmillan, 1987.

Brooks, William. *Speech Communications* 4th ed. Dubuque, IA.: Wm. C. Brown Co., 1981.

Casagrande, D., and R. Casagrande. *Oral Communication in Technical Professions and Businesses*. Belmont, CA: Wadsworth, 1986.

Cronkhite, Gary. *Public Speaking and Critical Listening*. Menlo Park, CA: The Benjamin/ Cummings Publishing Co., Inc., 1978.

DeVito, Joseph. *The Elements of Public Speaking* 3d ed. New York: Harper & Row, 1987.

Ehninger, D., B. Gronbeck and A. Monroe. *Principles of Speech Communication* 9th ed. Glenview, IL: Scott, Foresman, 1984.

Gronbeck, B. *The Articulate Person: A Guide to Everyday Public Speaking*. Glenview, IL: Scott, Foresman, 1983.

Howell, William, and Ernest Bormann. *Presentational Speaking for Business and the Professions*. New York: Harper & Row, 1971.

Hugenberg, L., and D. Yoder. *Speaking in the Modern Organization: Skills and Strategies*. Glenview, IL: Scott, Foresman, 1984.

Raudsepp, Eugene, and Joseph C. Yeager. *How to Sell New Ideas*. Englewood Cliffs, NJ: Prentice-Hall, 1981.

Reid, Loren. *Speaking Well* 4th ed. New York: McGraw-Hill Book Co., 1982.

Sprague, Jo, and Douglas Stuart. *The Speaker's Handbook*. New York: Harcourt Brace Jovanovich, 1984.

Verderber, Rudolph F. *The Challenge of Effective Speaking* 6th ed. Belmont, CA: Wadsworth Publishing Co., 1985.

Communication

Barker, Larry L. *Listening Behavior*. Englewood Cliffs, NJ: Prentice-Hall, 1971.

Conrad, C. *Strategic Organizational Communication*. New York: Holt, Rinehart, and Winston, 1985.

Daniels, T., and B. Spiker. *Perspectives on Organizational Communication*. Dubuque, IA: William C. Brown, 1987.

Donaghy, W. *The Interview: Skills and Applications*. Glenview, IL: Scott, Foresman, 1984.

Goldhaber, Gerald M. *Organizational Communication* 4th ed. Dubuque, IA: Wm. C. Brown Co., 1986.

Hall, Edward T. *The Hidden Dimension*. Garden City, NY: Doubleday, 1966.

Haney, William V. *Communication and Organizational Behavior*. Homewood, IL: Richard D. Irwin, Inc. 1973.

Hunt, G., and W. Eadiem. *Interviewing: A Communication Approach*. New York: Holt, Rinehart, and Winston, 1987.

Jablin, F., L. Putnam, K. Roberts, and L. Porter, eds. *Handbook of Organizational Communication*. Beverly, Hills, CA: Sage, 1987.

Knapp, Mark L. *Nonverbal Communication in Human Interaction*. New York: Holt, Rinehart and Winston, 1978.

Kreps, Gary L. *Organizational Communication*. New York: Longman, 1986.

Mehrabian, Albert. *Silent Messages*. Belmont, CA: Wadsworth Publishing Co., 1971.

Reardon, K. *Interpersonal Communication: Where Minds Meet*. Belmont, CA: Wadsworth, 1987.

Redding, W. C. *Communication within the Organization.* New York: Industrial Communications Council and Lafayette, IN, Purdue Research Foundation, 1972.

Reuss, C., and D. Silvis. International Association of Business Communicators. *Inside Organizational Communication* 2d. ed. New York: Longman, 1985.

Weaver, Carl H. *Human Listening: Processes and Behavior.* New York: Bobbs-Merrill Co., 1972.

Wilmot, W. *Dyadic Communication* 3d ed. New York: Random House, 1987.

Wolvin, A., and C. Coakley. *Listening* 2d ed. Dubuque, IA: William C. Brown, 1985.

Group Dynamics

Bales, Robert Freed. *Personality and Interpersonal Behavior.* New York: Holt, Rinehart and Winston, 1970.

Benne, K. D., and P. Sheats. "Functional Roles of Group Members." *Journal of Social Issues* 4, (1948): 41–49.

Bormann, Ernest G. *Discussion and Group Methods: Theory and Practice,* New York: Harper & Row, 1975.

Cartwright, Dorwin, and Alvin Zander, ed. *Group Dynamics: Research and Theory.* New York: Harper & Row, 1968.

Cathcart, Robert S., and Larry A. Samovar. *Small Group Communication: A Reader* 3d ed. Dubuque, IA: Wm. C. Brown Co., 1979.

Filley, Alan C. *Interpersonal Conflict Resolution.* Glenview, IL: Scott, Foresman, 1975.

Gibb, J. "Defensive Communication." *Journal of Communication* 11 (1961): 141–48.

Goodall, H. *Small Group Communication in Organizations.* Dubuque, IA: William C. Brown, 1985.

Ofshe, Richard J., ed. *Interpersonal Behavior in Small Groups.* Englewood Cliffs, NJ: Prentice-Hall, 1973.

Schutz, W. *FIRO: A Three-Dimensional Theory of Interpersonal Behavior.* New York: Holt, Rinehart and Winston, 1958.

Shaw, Marvin E. *Group Dynamics: The Psychology of Small Group Behavior* 3d ed. New York: McGraw-Hill Book Co., 1981.

Tuckman, Bruce W. "Developmental Sequence in Small Groups." *Psychological Bulletin* 63, No. 6 (1965).

Wood, J., G. Phillips, and D. Pedersen. *Group Discussion: A Practical Guide to Participation and Leadership.* New York: Harper & Row, 1986.

Team Leadership

Argyris, C. *Increasing Leadership Effectiveness.* Melbourne, FL: Krieger Publishing, 1983.

Blake, Robert R., and Jane Srygley Mouton. *The New Managerial Grid.* Houston: Gulf Publishing Co., 1978.

Hersey, Paul, and Ken Blanchard. *Management of Organizational Behavior: Utilizing Human Resources* 4th ed. Englewood Cliffs, NJ: Prentice-Hall, 1982.

Likert, Rensis. *New Patterns of Management.* New York: McGraw-Hill Book Co., 1961.

Odiorne, George S. *MBO II: A System of Managerial Leadership for the 80s,* Belmont, CA: Fearon Pitman Publishers, 1979.

Peters, Tom, and Nancy Austin. *A Passion for Excellence: The Leadership Difference.* New York: Random House, 1985.

Scheidel, Thomas, and Laura Crowell. *Discussing and Deciding: A Desk Book for Group Leaders and Members.* New York: Macmillan, 1979.

Tannenbaum, R., and W. Schmidt. "How to Choose a Leadership Pattern." *Harvard Business Review* 36 (1958): 95–101.

CHAPTER 4

Quality Improvement Teams in Action

Basic Structures

A team usually consists of three to eleven voluntary members who have a shared area of responsibility. Historically, the work function of the members is at a lower level, although there are some teams composed of managerial personnel. The members meet on a regular basis and receive training in problem identification, analysis techniques, and skills that help them improve quality and productivity in their area.

The leader of a team is usually the work area supervisor. It is the responsibility of the leader to train members with the assistance of the facilitator, to ensure the smooth and effective operation of the team, and to involve all members at each meeting. In addition to problem identification, analysis, and measurement skills, the leader also receives training in group dynamics, leadership skills, and communication.

The organizational facilitator or coordinator is often on the staff of a company official who is a strong supporter of team activities. This overall coordinator organizes and works with the teams on a gradually decreasing basis until the groups are self-directing and self-perpetuating. The coordinator may train the team leaders and departmental facilitators. In addition, the coordinator assists the leader in training members. When technical experts must be called in to assist the team, it is the coordinator who arranges this assistance, and ensures that the experts act only as consultants, rather than take control of team activities. Helping the leader and members communicate the results of their efforts to management and the organization is the responsibility of the coordinator. This person also must coordinate the publication of team progress in outside journals, as well as in-house publications.

In large or complex organizations, it may be necessary to select departmental facilitators. In this case, the departmental facilitator is on the staff of the head of the department or division where teams are implemented. This person reports to the department head for appraisal and salary, but reports to the overall coordinator on team activities, progress, and assistance. The departmental facilitator works closely with departmental teams on training and problem solving. It is important that the departmental facilitator's responsibilities are kept detailed and separate from those of the coordinator to minimize overlap in their functions. Both must be capable of being promoter, coach, teacher, coordinator, and liaison between all levels of management and employees.

The last essential element of the quality team organizational structure is the steering or advisory committee. It is composed of managers and top staff personnel, and includes the coordinator. The committee's purpose is to set general objectives and goals for the process and to establish operational guidelines and the rate of expansion. The steering committee also chooses departmental facilitators as needed, and determines funding arrangements for group training and activities. In addition, the steering committee has the responsibility for publicizing, promoting, and educating people about the approach and progress as well as joining in celebration of the team's success. A chairperson presides over the democratic processes of the committee.

After this organizational structure has been established for pilot groups and the quality team approach has been approved by senior level management, implementation and operation begin.

Implementation starts with an explanation of the employee involvement concept to management and to employees. All levels of management must be involved. The go-ahead for teams comes from upper management, but the approval goes through a filter of many levels before it reaches the employees. The first step in the process, after receiving approval, is to familiarize upper management and the steering committee with participative philosophy and techniques. It is crucial at this point that steering committee members thoroughly understand the implications of team activities and the role the steering committee must play in gaining support and enthusiasm from supervisors and employees. To facilitate this process, it is recommended that managers receive a formal orientation to employee involvement concepts and detailed training on problem-solving techniques, so they have a clear understanding of the purpose and goals of the teams. The next step is to consider specifically what actions managers should take to express their support of the process publicly and heighten awareness of the participative concept among the work force. Simply approving the process is not enough. Managers must provide evidence to employees that teams will be supported on a day-to-day basis. Once upper management thoroughly understands and openly supports the team process, acceptance and implementation can be facilitated. By allowing the work force the opportunity to become involved in making decisions about their jobs, management is voicing support and commitment to participation concepts that the employees do have something valuable to contribute to improve both themselves and the organization as a whole.

As discussed in the previous chapter, leaders and facilitators are often trained in extensive three-day courses that include modules in problem identification, analysis, measurement techniques, and presentation skills, as well as training in group dynamics, leadership, and communication. The leaders and facilitators help present the approach to the employees and request volunteers. It is important at this point to make sure the potential members are adequately oriented to employee involvement concepts so they can make an informed decision about participation. The more orientation the better (e.g., two one-hour sessions as opposed to one half-hour session). Once potential members have decided to join, the leader then trains the volunteers in useful and relevant problem-solving tools and measurement techniques. Typically, the teams meet for one hour per week. This can be during regular working hours, overtime, or on the employees' own time, with or without pay, depending on what works best for each organization. However, allowing meetings during working hours is evidence that management believes in and supports the process. The meeting agenda is divided with half of the time spent training members, and half devoted to problem identification, analysis, and recommendation.

The problem-solving and measurement techniques taught to team members, leaders, and facilitators vary. The new skills acquired through this instruction are useful for problem solving in team activities as well as for personal development outside the group. The tools and skills of planning and controlling projects, brainstorming, sampling, surveying, flow charting, work measurement, work simplification, project cost and benefit analysis, and presentation techniques are the core modules taught to all people involved in quality team activities.

When group members receive sufficient training and become somewhat self-directed, assistance from and contact with the facilitator declines. Occasional training refreshers are given by the facilitator to keep the newly-learned skills sharp. Some projects will require the use of all the techniques to solve the problem or to make improvements. Others may require the use of only one or two. The techniques are tools that are used by teams, when appropriate, to tackle work-related problems and develop improvements. The order in which they are presented is a guide, not a rule. The facilitator, leader, and team members decide which tools they can use to complete each project successfully.

Brainstorming

Brainstorming is one of the most effective and frequently used tools. This creative method involves working in a group to stimulate the production of ideas. It is useful for identifying potential projects for the group, determining a team nickname, or isolating elements for problem analysis. The brainstorming sessions should be enjoyable, as well as productive. The effectiveness of brainstorming in unlocking the creative power of the group has long been recognized. The team process is more effective than trying to generate ideas alone. Visitors and nonmembers may participate in brainstorming sessions, but the rules of brainstorming must be stated clearly to avoid embarrassment or misunderstanding.

Before beginning, it is vital that the team identifies what topic will be brainstormed. The leader should be as precise as possible in stating the topic to be brainstormed. For example, "Productivity Problems Within Our Work Area" as a topic is better than simply stating "Productivity," which is too general. The topic should be stated clearly and specifically so members will not lose time and effort.

Brainstorming works best when certain guidelines are followed. The leader should review these prior to every brainstorming session so team members become familiar with them. Round-robin brainstorming is often useful to ensure more equal participation. The following brainstorming rules are used for this procedure:

- Each member, in rotation, is asked for ideas. This continues until all ideas have been exhausted.

- Each member offers only one idea per turn.

- Not everyone has an idea during each rotation. When this occurs, the member says, "Pass."

- During brainstorming, no evaluation of suggested ideas—positive or negative—should occur. This rule applies equally to the leader.

- No idea should be treated as silly or wrong. To criticize or belittle someone will curtail the creativity of team members.

After the rules have been explained, the brainstorming session can begin. This process will be more useful if one member, serving as recorder, writes the ideas as they are given. The leader, or the recorder, will often have to abbreviate a lengthy idea into a few words, but the originator must agree. During the brainstorming session, strive for a large quantity of ideas to maximize the effectiveness of the process.

For some, this will be their first attempt to speak during a brainstorming session and it may take a while to get started. All ideas, no matter how exaggerated, should be encouraged. Exaggeration may be humorous, but it adds a creative stimulus to the process. Likewise, a touch of fantasy can help shed the bonds that prevent members from thinking creatively. Examples of this might be imagining that the laws of gravity are cancelled or making some connection between totally unrelated items.

Brainstorming is complete when all ideas have been exhausted. This occurs when all members have passed in one complete round. Next, the ideas must be examined critically and narrowed through a discussion, ranking, and voting process.

After the actual brainstorming session, members get involved in a discussion period where ideas are clarified and similar concepts combined. Team members should feel free to explain their ideas or ask for clarification so that the group has a good understanding of all ideas generated. However, at this point, no idea should be eliminated unless it is being combined with a similar idea. If an idea is thought to be irrelevant or unrelated, this will be decided during the voting process.

Once the discussion of ideas is complete, the team begins a voting process to condense and rank the list of ideas generated. Members vote on each idea. The recorder lists the number of votes. During the first round of voting, members can vote for as many ideas as they believe have value. Only supporting votes are taken; no one is asked to vote against an idea. After the first round of voting, each member may vote for only one idea to conclude the voting and finalize the top priorities. If the list is lengthy, the members may wish to have two or three more rounds of voting to establish the final priority ranking. The leader will decide a cutoff point after the first round (i.e., the five items receiving the most votes). The recorder then circles these items as well as the number of votes (preferably in a different color). The members then will be able to focus on a few important items.

To obtain a priority ranking, a final round of voting is conducted and members vote for the one idea they believe has the most value. The recorder writes the ranking number beside each item that has been circled and puts a box around it to indicate the number one, number two, and number three priority items.

After a problem has been identified and analyzed, team members join in a brainstorming session to determine ways to verify the true cause of the problem as well as possible solutions.

Problem prevention analysis can be a productive activity as well. Brainstorming helps clarify potential difficulties and may even prevent them from becoming bigger problems in the future.

Incubation often occurs after the initial brainstorming session. "Let's sleep on it" is a frequently voiced comment. Later, many innovative ideas may emerge. To facilitate this process, the brainstorming record should be posted in the work area when possible. The chart will receive a lot of attention and ideas may be added to it during the week. A legend should be included on all charts to identify the team and leader's name, and the date the chart was constructed. Such information is vital for historical and reference value at a future date.

Planning

An objective is described as the desired outcome of the project, or a general statement of what is to be accomplished. Plans are structured schemes or projections of what the team wants to have happen in the future. Goals are specific targets within the plan to reach team objectives. There are guidelines that assist in setting goals. A number of techniques are also available to help monitor and control progress toward these goals. The best method for achieving results is to follow these steps:

■ Determine objectives

■ Develop a plan for reaching objectives

■ Set goals and identify action items within this plan

■ Monitor and control progress

Achieving positive results is the desired outcome of any team project. No one wants to start something that cannot be finished in a way that meets expectations. Almost everyone has been frustrated by wasting valuable time in meetings, not fulfilling responsibilities, or not accomplishing tasks. The best method of avoiding this frustration is to decide specifically what the team wants to accomplish, how the team can accomplish it, and what actions are required. Objectives should be concise and brief. These statements summarize the major focus of the project. Although objectives can be measurable, they do not include dates, deadlines, assigned tasks, responsibilities for personnel, or quantities. For example, a problem may be user complaints about timeliness; the team objective would be to improve turnaround time for reports. Once a definite objective has been determined, a plan must be developed to reach it.

The next step in planning involves examining alternative courses of action to accomplish the objectives. This examination should not exclude any possibilities, especially those not immediately apparent. Determining the specific steps that must be taken involves establishing sound goals for the team project. Goals are short-range targets within a plan that contain measurable achievements within specified time periods. Unlike objectives, specific guidelines may be given for setting meaningful goals.

The following guidelines are quite simple; however, it takes considerable time and practice to develop concise, purposeful goals. People are sometimes hesitant to monitor their own performance, and may prefer to write loose goal statements. Vague goal statements can be a major problem in the planning process. Developing goals that are consistent with these guidelines can assure that team plans are completed.

Goals Should Be Specific. The more specific a goal is, the more useful it becomes. Goals identify precisely what is to be done and when it is to be accomplished. Details and dates should always be included.

Goals Should Be Measurable. Goals are intended to be a yardstick, against which performance of an individual or team can be evaluated. If performance is to be verified, it is necessary to state goals in an objective, comparative way.

Goals Should Be Results-centered. Whenever possible, focus on the results to be accomplished, not the activities to accomplish them. Activity is the means of getting there, not the end that is sought. Teams must avoid the tendency to view performance in terms of ongoing tasks, rather than results.

Goals Should Be Realistic. Goals must be feasible and attainable. Optimism that too much can be done too soon, can hurt the team project; deadlines will be missed, work will be left incomplete, and enthusiasm will lag. Realistic goals are those within the bounds or control of the team setting them.

Goals Should Be Challenging. Goals can be realistic and encourage high levels of performance as well. Setting aims high can motivate the team to achieve results, expand its capabilities and develop greater improvements. Goals should call for improved performance, but not be so high as to be discouraging.

Goals Should Be Flexible. Goals need not be rigid. Teams should not adhere to goals blindly, but rather change them if conditions dictate. However, continual altering of goals and deadlines will result in impractical plans and poor performance.

Goals Should Be Limited in Number. The team should not be confused by too many goals. Concentrating only on what needs to be done will eliminate distracting and time-wasting tasks.

Groups Involved in Accomplishing the Goals Should Participate in the Establishment of the Goals. Participation in developing goals will promote a feeling of ownership and a commitment to achieving them. If people are given a say in the way something is to be done, they will be less likely to criticize or reject the plan.

There are many simple techniques that can be used to achieve the goals the team has set. The first of these is a chart of the basic activities required to accomplish a particular goal. Commonly, these are referred to as *action logs*. They identify the goals that must be met to achieve team objectives and list the activities required to accomplish each specific goal including pertinent details. Usually several actions are required; goals are seldom accomplished in a single step. The team members responsible for each job are listed, and targeted completion dates are noted in the log.

Action logs facilitate the planning process by making team goals more explicit. Written target dates and related activities motivate teams and individuals to complete tasks and accomplish objectives. Commitment to the project is encouraged through the assignment of tasks to appropriate personnel. Figure 4.1 is an example of a basic activity log for a project to improve turnaround time. Note that while the team works on all aspects of the project, certain individuals are responsible for the coordination of specific tasks.

In project planning and controlling, it is important that when a project is selected some expectations or parameters are set. The project should be divided into small

FIGURE 4.1

ACTION ITEMS FOR: Improved Turnaround Time Project

Goals	Activities	Person Responsible	Dates Target	Actual
■ Determine current turnaround time	■ Collect/organize turnaround data from last two weeks ■ Analyze this information	Mike	Week 1	
■ Identify ways to shorten turnaround time	■ Basic cause and effect on "high turnaround time" ■ Brainstorm verification of causes; then verify	Jennifer Kari	Weeks 2–6	
■ Develop recommendations	■ Brief division staff ■ Brainstorm possible solutions ■ Select/document recommendation	Kim	Weeks 7–8	
■ Present recommendations to managers	■ Develop presentation ■ Rehearse presentation ■ Management presentation	Leader	Weeks 9–11	

units or tasks. This allows the team to determine how much time will be needed for each portion of the project, what resources are required, and the time frames in which each task should be accomplished.

An easy way to develop a project plan and measure progress is to construct a *Gantt chart* of the individual tasks or steps that need to be completed for the project. This bar-type diagram lists the known steps that need to be accomplished on the left side. A time line along the bottom indicates the total time for the project from the beginning to the end. For each of the steps a time frame should be estimated based on the amount of work that needs to be done, the number of people who are going to be working on that particular step, and their available time. For each step, a block is drawn starting with the date the activity should begin and ending with the date the activity should be completed. The team should consider the number of hours to complete each step and the number of hours that can be allocated to complete that step.

By looking at the steps in the project the team will be able to assess whether the activities can be completed sequentially—or simultaneously. Those activities that can be completed simultaneously will reduce the total project calendar time if team members are assigned to do different steps at the same time. The Gantt chart will allow team members to know when they should start different steps and when they should complete tasks, assuming that the time estimates are realistic. By charting a second block underneath each planning block indicating the time the task was started, the time actually spent on the project, and when the project was actually completed, the team can get a sense of whether the steps are being completed on time. If the deadlines are not being met, additional resources may be needed or the time frames may need to be adjusted. Projects should be planned so that they run no more than three to six months.

Measuring projects in this way has proven effective in reducing project time by up to fifty percent. Failures are also reduced because teams do not become frustrated in carrying out the project ineffectively. A sample Gantt chart of team activities from collecting and organizing data on a specific project to making the management presentation is shown (Figure 4.2).

A major step in achieving results is the follow-up on planning. This phase involves monitoring and controlling team progress in relation to planned objectives. Monitoring requires measuring, checking, or overseeing a process. Control refers to the management or regulation of this process. Keeping a watch on team progress allows the team to determine where it is in reference to where it wants to be. Then the team can more easily overcome obstacles and reevaluate plans. It is easier to control progress once current project status is determined. Is the team ahead of schedule? Behind schedule? Is anyone neglecting responsibilities? Has some barrier hindered the total process or project?

Feedback is also a useful method of control. Letting those involved know the project status can help control future performance. Visually displaying progress on a Gantt chart emphasizes the importance of keeping on schedule and achieving results.

FIGURE 4.2

Sample Gantt Chart

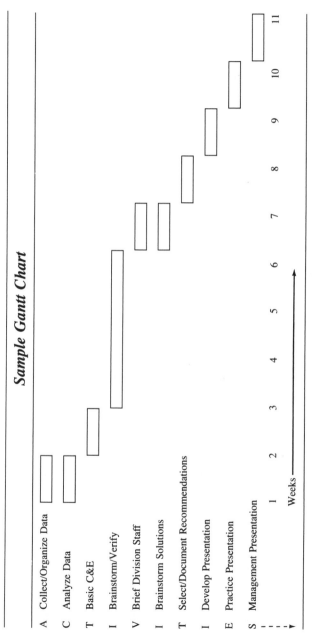

A Collect/Organize Data

C Analyze Data

T Basic C&E

I Brainstorm/Verify

V Brief Division Staff

I Brainstorm Solutions

T Select/Document Recommendations

I Develop Presentation

E Practice Presentation

S Management Presentation

Weeks   1   2   3   4   5   6   7   8   9   10   11

Recognition for completion of individual tasks is another way to control the process. Acknowledgment of a job well done encourages high levels of team performance. Unsatisfactory completion of tasks should also be recognized and followed up to keep the project on track.

Of course such changes may require a modified, or possibly a new, overall plan. The team should avoid the tendency to make changes when the schedule is not met. This often leads to indifference toward planning and performance, and lack of thoroughness in thinking through original plans. Changing the plan is the last alternative that should be considered. There are usually many other options, e.g., making up time on the next objective, collecting less data, or skipping an insignificant step. Careful planning and monitoring can help the team to complete projects in a timely, satisfying manner.

Flow Charting

Flow charting is a useful problem-solving technique for teams and managers. A flow chart is a means of portraying, in graphic form, a sequence of specified operations performed on identified items of output, information, or documents that are handled routinely. Flow charts are composed of boxes or outlines of various shapes with connecting arrows and flow lines. There are five basic outlines to symbolize fundamental steps in processes. Appropriate combinations of these outlines build flow charts that depict a specific process.

The Start or End Outline. This is a horizontal oval. All procedures have a beginning and a finish. Only two of these outlines are used in any one process: one at the beginning and one at the end. ◯

The Input or Output Outline. This is a parallelogram; the vertical lines are angled to give the illusion of movement. Usually the input source or destination is written inside of the outline. ▱

The Process Outline. This is the general purpose outline that indicates a transformation, movement, step, or process in the operation. It is the most common of the outlines, and is shaped like a simple rectangle. □

The Decision Outline. The flow diagram depicts situations requiring a choice in processing. The decision outline is diamond-shaped with the alternative paths clearly marked. ◇

Connectors. These are circles that are used to show entering or leaving the process. These entrances or exits may be used as part of the logical process or to avoid crossing lines in the flow diagram on a particular page. Typically, connectors are labeled with letters to indicate where to leave off and where to pick up. Connectors also indicate that the remainder of a flow diagram may be found on another page or sheet. ◯

When the team members are familiar with the outlines they can begin to draw the process diagram. The first step and the simplest approach is to write a short verbal description of what the process entails. For example, "Sales slips are received in batches. Totals on sales slips are inputted to the CRT. Totals are run on the CRT and balanced. Balanced batches are sent to the Payment Section.''

The next step is to underline those words in the description that best describe the individual steps of the process. These can be used as guidelines for the flow diagram outlines. In this example, the words "received batches," "inputted to CRT," "balanced," and "sent" should be underlined. Notice that these words describe the most basic tasks or actions required to complete the operations.

Next, the team uses the appropriate symbol for each of the underlined phrases keeping them in sequence. They fill in the process outlines with summaries that are clear, consistent, and brief. The team includes information or details that members believe are important. The verbal description provides the guideline for the remaining outlines. Notice that the primary functions of an area are highlighted by the flow chart; supporting tasks may not be included in the flow diagram overview. Details, such as the person responsible for the function or locations, may be added above or below outlines and flowlines. The illustration (Table 4.1) shows how the operations of an area may be shown on a flow chart.

The following is a list of guidelines for drawing clear, uniform flow charts:

■ A flow diagram that is simple and clean communicates specific operations much better than one that is cluttered or lacks "white space."

■ The flow pattern of outlines should be from top to bottom and from left to right.

■ Entrances should be drawn at the upper left and exits at the lower right.

■ Flow lines are drawn so that the lines enter and exit at the visual centers of the outlines.

■ Flow lines should not be crossed within the diagram. Connectors should be used instead.

There are many creative applications of this technique. For example, flow diagrams can be used to simplify work. Once each function has been reviewed, those steps that are not essential may be eliminated. Another use of the flow diagram is to combine tasks. Perhaps everyone has a specialized function, but tasks are repetitive and boring. If all tasks required to process a piece of work were performed by each individual, the job might be more interesting and challenging.

Is everyone located in the work area in the most logical place? Diagramming the physical flow of work may indicate a more efficient floor plan. A flow diagram of operations can serve as a guideline for discussion or brainstorming of actual or potential problems in an area. These problems can then be analyzed and monitored. Clear and concise flow diagrams can help the team define a specific work process, explain it to others in an easy-to-understand format, and improve area operations and individual job responsibilities.

TABLE 4.1

A *communications distribution center* receives corporate information from other sections that must be typed and sent to outside customers. The *supervisor receives* the information from *"user divisions"* (i.e., those divisions that depend on the center for service) in the form of *letters, memos,* and *special mailings by messenger.* The supervisor *fills* out a *work requisition* and *project fact sheet* and gives all of the materials to the word processing (w.p.) coordinator. The *coordinator adds information* to the project fact sheet and *distributes the material* to be typed to the *w.p. specialist.* After *typing the information,* the w.p. specialist *returns the work* to the coordinator. The *coordinator* again *adds pertinent information* to the project *fact sheet* and *returns* the sheet with the typed materials to the *supervisor.* The *supervisor checks* the work, *copies* it, and *distributes* it with the fact sheet to mailing clerks. *Mailing clerks prepare the copies for mailing* and *send them to customers* per instructions on the fact sheet. Fact sheets are *returned* to the *supervisor,* who *files them* and the *requisitions.*

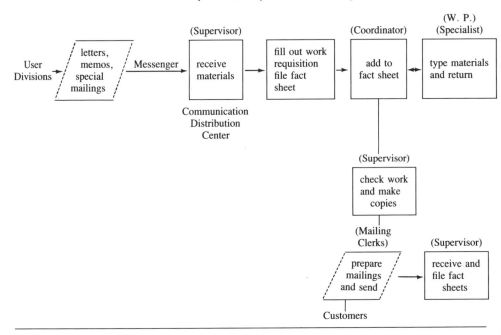

Sampling

When sampling, the team investigates a portion of the whole to make decisions or inferences about the whole. Taking an appropriate sample saves time and money and allows a more accurate investigation of the data. Three ways to sample data are by random selection, systematic selection, and stratified selection of data. When applying sampling techniques to business operations, the methods must be scientific and precise. The team attempts to draw conclusions about a large group of individuals or elements by collecting information from a small portion of that whole.

There are many areas in which to use sampling techniques. Many teams decide to keep track of the efficiency or error rates of the processes and functions performed in their work areas. They want to ensure that the "product" of their work area is of sufficiently high quality before it goes to the internal or external customer. Sampling may be used by the team in researching a particular problem in the work area and finding the source or cause. Sampling is a helpful tool that assists in the collection of data for a variety of purposes.

Before deciding to sample rather than make a one hundred percent inspection, the team must be aware of the advantages and disadvantages of each. Sampling has several advantages over complete inspection. First of all, it is obviously less time consuming. Particularly when information is needed urgently, sampling allows the data to be collected and analyzed much more quickly than a complete count. Because sampling requires less time, it is also less costly in terms of human effort. Sometimes the cost of a complete inspection of a group is prohibitive, and the team must resort to taking a sample.

An often overlooked advantage of sampling is that it generally allows a more comprehensive and accurate inspection of the elements observed. When a person has more time to inspect something, there is less possibility of overlooking errors. A one hundred percent inspection on average will only yield eighty-seven percent accuracy. Individually inspecting all of the items is extremely tedious. Records from such inspections are often full of inaccuracies due to the fatigue of the inspector.

However, there is a risk involved when sampling. Whenever the team attempts to draw inferences about a large group of elements by observing only a portion of the elements, it runs the risk of being mistaken in its conclusions. When there is a possibility that a sample contains a disproportionately high amount of defective elements, the team is led to believe that the total group of elements has a high defective rate. Conversely, the team can be lulled into a false sense of security by a sample that has a low percentage of errors as compared to the total group. In situations where the cost of even one undetected error is extremely great, careful one hundred percent inspection may be mandatory to avoid the risk. Yet some errors still will not be detected and multiple inspections could be required.

In short, when trying to decide whether or not to sample in lieu of making a total inspection, the team must weigh the advantages of savings in time, effort, and cost against the risk involved. Every situation has unique factors that will influence this decision. The decision will depend upon good judgment in weighing these factors. In most cases a sample is sufficient.

A sample is selected from a group of items referred to as a *population*. Before starting to sample, the population should be clearly defined as to the elements it contains and its limits or boundaries. For instance, "checks encoded by our entire section within a given week" is a better definition of a particular population than "checks encoded."

The numerical characteristics of a population are called *parameters*, while those of a sample are called *statistics*. In selecting a sample, the team attempts to choose elements whose characteristics, as a group, will be representative of the population and its parameters. For example, if the actual average daily rate of encoding errors for the previously mentioned population is 0.3 percent, the sample should also have an average error rate of 0.3 percent.

The characteristic of the sample should represent the values of the population as closely as possible. Whenever the average value of the sample deviates from that of its population, *bias* occurs. Bias should be avoided since it reduces the ability to make accurate predictions about the population based on data collected from the sample.

Bias can occur in a variety of ways. Suppose a team wants to know the average length of teller lines between 9:00 A.M. and 5:00 P.M. to determine whether there is an adequate number of tellers. If the team takes a sample count daily for five days straight during the peak hour of noon to 1:00 P.M., results will surely be biased; the sample will not reflect the population.

Another example might be a team that checks the average computer input error rate in the work area on a continuous basis to keep track of quality improvement. If samples are taken from the work of only two of ten operators, the data will most likely be biased.

Accessibility must be considered when attempting to select an unbiased sample; each element of the population should have an equal chance of being chosen. Choosing those elements that are most easily located will almost surely result in bias. Consider a team at a bank that conducts a telephone survey to explore the attitudes of demand deposit customers toward their bank. People are telephoned only between the hours of 8:00 A.M. and 5:00 P.M. This means a majority of the sample will be homemakers or people who are not employed during regular work hours. Such an easily accessible sample will certainly not be representative of the entire population of demand deposit customers.

The team can avoid bias and help to assure that its sample is representative of the population by following the correct methods. Three commonly used methods of sampling are random, systematic, and stratified sampling. The type that is most applicable depends on the characteristics of the population and other factors.

Random Sampling. This is a method in which each population element has an equal chance of being chosen, and the selection of any one element does not affect the selection of any other element. It is probably easiest to illustrate the principle of random sampling by citing some examples of nonrandom samples. Taking the top twenty-five forms from each stack of one hundred forms is not a random selection, since not all the forms have an equal chance of being chosen. Similarly, choosing every third form from a stack of one hundred technically would not be a random sample, since the selection of one element serves to determine the selection of another.

Random sampling helps protect against bias and aids in the selection of a truly representative sample. Random sampling is usually done with the use of a random numbers table. Such a table should be used for selecting a random sample of any population that contains items numbered from one to n (n being the total size of the population). This process assures randomness, but can be time-consuming.

Systematic Sampling. In this method the selection of an item from a population is based on a constant fixed interval between each item and the next item in the population. For instance, choosing every fifth account from a computer printout of customer accounts would be an example of systematic sampling.

Certain conditions must be met for this type of sampling to be effective. The items in the population itself must be distributed randomly, in regard to the characteristics to be observed in the sample. For instance, an alphabetical listing of customer accounts generally would be considered random if the team is sampling errors in the posting of interest. Suppose that one operator posts the interest for accounts A through K while the rest of the alphabet is handled by two other operators. All these operators differ in the degree of accuracy of their work. In this case, an alphabetical listing would be considered nonrandom for systematic sampling purposes.

Another requirement for systematic sampling is that no items of the population be missing. When selecting this type of sample, the team should start at any random point in the population, and proceed until the entire sample has been collected. For example, when using a printout of customer accounts to draw a systematic sample, the team simply flips through the printout and stops at any arbitrary point to use it as a starting place.

Stratified Sampling. This refers to a sample in which the items of the population are grouped into two or more categories, and the items within each population category are selected randomly according to the proportion they represent within the population. Stratified sampling is a useful tool for sampling populations with a wide variety of item values. By using this technique, pollsters are often able to make remarkably accurate predictions based on extremely small samples.

Stratified sampling can be helpful in the office as well. For example, consider the alphabetical listing of customer accounts. Assume Karl handles A through K (fifty percent of the accounts), Bill handles L through R (twenty-five percent), and Connie handles S through Z (twenty-five percent). The team wishes to find out the average error rate in posting interest, but knows that the operators vary in the accuracy of their work, so the team decides to stratify the sample. There are a total of two thousand accounts, and the team decides to take a sample of six hundred (thirty percent of the total number). The team selects three hundred of Karl's accounts (fifty percent), and one hundred fifty each of Bill's and Connie's (twenty-five percent each).

Since the team members believe the accounts are distributed randomly within these categories, they use the systematic method of sampling to obtain a random sample within each group, choosing every third item until the total sample is collected. This investigation reveals a two percent error rate in the posting of interest on accounts within the samples. The team feels safe in predicting that the error rate is about the same for the total number of accounts.

Regardless of which method of sampling is used, choosing the size of the sample can be a complex matter if strict scientific principles are followed. These are some basic guidelines. In general, if the population is greater than one hundred, a sample size of thirty percent is usually adequate. If the population is extremely large, the group should refer to a sampling table. If the population is less than one hundred, a greater percentage than thirty percent should be taken. In fact, if the population has fifty items or less, it may be a good idea to do a one hundred percent inspection, or something close to it. The team should follow these steps in sampling:

■ *Step 1*. Learn the facts of the population. For example, the team is polling people to forecast the use of a proposed computer system. Some things the team must consider are: What groups, administrative or operational, make up the department's population? Relative size of each? Average training in computer skills? Grade levels? Past usage trends? Educational levels? If the team wants the sample to represent the population, it needs to know basic characteristics of the population.

■ *Step 2*. Learn how large the population is. Population refers to the total number of items or people the team is interested in observing, and from which the sample will be drawn. In the case of the poll, the population is the total number of people who would potentially use the computer system.

■ *Step 3*. Choose the sample size. The team may want the help of staff experts who are skilled in sampling techniques.

■ *Step 4*. Select the sample. In the previous example, the team taking the poll decides what users would form a representative sample. The sample selected may contain users from all grade levels. This would be an example of stratified sample.

■ *Step 5*. Collect the data needed on each element of the sample. For instance, the team would ask each person in the sample carefully chosen questions regarding possible use of the computer system.

■ *Step 6*. A prediction is made based on the results of the sample. The word "prediction" is used because the team cannot be absolutely certain that the sample accurately reflects the condition of the entire population.

Following these steps will assure that the team has accurate information and that the information gathered about the sample truly reflects the characteristics of the population. The team obtains a large amount of important data with the least effort and cost.

Sampling techniques can be a helpful tool for teams in collecting data. If certain principles are strictly followed, samples can be remarkably accurate in predicting the characteristics of their corresponding populations. The data derived from sampling research can be used for a variety of purposes in quality and productivity improvement.

Survey Data Collection

Facts are most often used as a basis for conclusions. Recommendations on quality and productivity problems must be based on objective proof. Yet subjective data including opinions and attitudes are also critical in understanding these problems and issues. Subjective data can be more difficult to gather than numerical data because the approach is less straightforward, and often more difficult to record. Surveys are one method used to collect spoken or written information in an objective and organized manner. The team can conduct surveys by mail, telephone, or face-to-face. All of these types of survey data collection must follow general principles for reliability in their design and use. Each has some advantages and disadvantages.

Which type of survey is best suited to team needs for information? Unfortunately, there is no simple answer to this question. For example, face-to-face interviews typically will give a high assurance of obtaining a representative sample of the target group (e.g., if the team needs to survey security personnel, chances are good that they will be able to identify most survey subjects by their uniforms). Response rates and cooperation for long questionnaires are often higher for the face-to-face surveys, because it is unlikely that the person being interviewed will refuse to answer a few more questions. In addition, more complex questions can be asked since face-to-face interviews allow for clarification and elaboration of questions and responses.

However, face-to-face surveying has two major drawbacks. First, it may be difficult to get accurate information; the individual interviewer can distort the meaning of a question by stressing particular words or phrases, or the respondent may intentionally or unintentionally bias results by answering questions untruthfully. Many times the respondent may believe the interviewer wants a certain response and may or may not conform to this perspective. The respondent may be accompanied by a friend or family member and can be hesitant or less than frank with an "audience" present. Secondly, face-to-face interviews are costly. More time is needed to conduct the interviews and to follow up.

Telephone surveys parallel the advantages and disadvantages of face-to-face interviews because of the personal interaction involved. Unlike personal interviews, telephone surveys do not allow for as much complexity in questions. When asked to answer a tedious question or to remember and select from a long list of choices, respondents may hang up. Another crucial difference between these two types is that phone surveys are generally less expensive and less time-consuming to administer than face-to-face interviews.

Collecting information in written form differs significantly from face-to-face or phone methods. Although the team can be assured of ease in selecting a representative sample, there is a stronger potential for bias in the results. Questionnaires received in the mail may be completed by people other than those in the target group, or thrown away. Unless the person contacted has an interest in the project, response rate may be low. Written surveys will furnish the highest accuracy of responses of all three types, provided that the questions are written properly and understood by the respondent. People also tend to be honest when completing mail questionnaires because their responses are anonymous. In addition, this method of data collection is usually the most inexpensive to administer, but it also takes the most time to receive returns from respondents and does not provide a chance for follow-up.

The team must weigh the advantages and disadvantages of each method before selecting the type of survey it should use. Each method has certain strengths and weaknesses. Until the characteristics of each method are considered in relation to the topic, the people to be surveyed, and what the team needs to know, the question of which is best cannot be answered.

The team should consider the following when trying to determine which method is best for the project. What specific information does the team want? How much time does the team have to get this information? Who will be giving the information? How much information is required? What resources are available? Table 4.2 summarizes the benefits and limitations of the three basic survey techniques.

This summary can help teams analyze needs and resources and select the method that is right for them. Once the team has selected the appropriate method, members can begin to develop a survey format and questions. The first step in writing the survey is to identify the information needed. Questions can usually be classified as requesting one or more of the following types of information:

- What people say they feel: their *attitudes*.

- What people think is true: their *beliefs*.

- What people do: their *behavior*.

- What people are: their *attributes*.

It is important to understand the differences among these types; otherwise, the questions asked may obtain different information from that which is needed.

Attitudes describe how people feel about specific ideas, issues, people and policies. They are evaluative and may reflect respondents' emotional views. Words typically used in attitude questions indicate the direction and intensity of individual feelings from "strongly agree" to "strongly disagree."

Beliefs are assessments of what a person thinks is true or false. There is no implied goodness or badness in beliefs, but only a gauge of what someone thinks exists or does not exist. Choices that are usually found in belief questions include "correct vs. incorrect" or "accurate vs. inaccurate."

The third kind of information commonly obtained in surveys consists of reports about respondents' *behavior*. In these behavioral questions, people are asked to describe things they have or will experience physically and what they are doing currently or what they plan to do in the future.

Attributes are sometimes referred to as personal or "demographic" characteristics. Examples of frequently requested attributes are age, education, work, sex, race,

TABLE 4.2

Basic Survey Techniques

Technique	Description	Benefits	Limitations	Relative Cost	Relative Turnaround Time	Relative Staff Resources
Mail Survey	Self-administered questionnaire Mail with self-addressed, stamped envelope	Anonymity allows candid responses Reaches geographically dispersed respondents	Strong bias from non-responses Response bias (misunderstanding of questions) Sequence bias (respondents change answers in previous sections after responding to later questions)	Inexpensive	Slowest	Smallest
Telephone Interview	Random sample of respondents from designated geographic area Telephone calls may last 10 to 15 minutes	Efficiently obtains high number of respondents with minimum effort 80 to 90% response rate Anonymity allows candid responses	Time is limited Cannot use graphic samples Locations with no telephones are excluded	Less expensive	Fastest	Large
Personal Interview	Respondents randomly selected for interviews in their homes or offices Face-to-face situation Interviewer must secure respondent's permission in advance	Interviews can be lengthy Interviewer can probe more effectively Body language can be incorporated Visual supports can be used	May hinder candid participation Direct control of interviewers is difficult Sampling bias (people, locations may be avoided by interviewers for subjective reasons)	Expensive	Slow	Largest

and marital status. The usual purpose for collecting this information is to explore how the other kinds of information (i.e., attitudes, beliefs, and behavior) differ for people with various attributes.

When the team has determined the type of information needed from the respondents (i.e., attitudes, beliefs, behavior, and/or attributes), the second step in writing a survey is to determine the structure of the questions. There are three basic structures for survey questions, and each structure can be used for collecting information. Questions may be open-ended, close-ended, or partially close-ended.

Open-ended questions have no choices from which respondents can select their answer. The people taking the survey must create their own answers and state them in their own words. These questions are used to stimulate free thought, solicit suggestions, probe people's memories, and clarify positions. They give respondents a chance to vent frustrations and state strong opinions. However, open-ended questions can be demanding because they force those taking the survey to create, organize, and express personal thoughts. Another frequent disadvantage is that responses may be difficult to quantify. In analyzing the responses to the question, "What should be done to improve your work section?," there may be hundreds of different answers!

Answer choices are provided for *close-ended questions*. Responses can be ordered with different numerical levels, e.g., "How long have you been in your current job?" a. Under four months, b. five to nine months, or c. over nine months; or responses may be separate, unordered categories to rank or select from, for example, "Which function takes the longest?" a. opening envelopes, b. batching advices, or c. sending wires.

Responses for attitude questions are generally close-ended with scales of the desirability or intensity of feeling. For example, responses may range from "definitely agree" to "somewhat agree" to "somewhat disagree" to "definitely disagree." To force the respondent to take a stance on a particular issue, rather than take the middle ground, the team can eliminate the "no opinion" choice.

Close-ended questions frequently are used in surveys because they are less demanding of the respondent than open-ended questions, and the results are generally easier to score. Choices are often given values that can then be totaled. A major disadvantage of the close-ended question is that the team must have enough knowledge of the topic to generate meaningful choices if the results are to be useful. Another related disadvantage is that respondents may believe that the best or most correct response is not listed as a choice. However, this problem can be solved by using a third type of question structure, the *partially close-ended question*. Such questions provide a compromise. Although answer choices are provided, respondents have the option of creating their own. An unordered, close-ended question can be turned into one that is only partially closed by adding the word "other." For example, "What is the biggest cause of work flow delay?" a. poor instructions, b. system downtime, c. unequal distribution of work, or d. other _____.

Using all three types of question structures in one survey can make the questionnaire more interesting. However, using the same structure throughout can save time in writing a survey and scoring the results. It is important to weigh the advantages and disadvantages of each type before selecting the structure that will help the team obtain needed information.

After the team has determined what type of information is needed and how it will be requested, the most important decision remains—how to word the questions. The same question must be uniformly understood by all of the survey respondents. For example, "Are personnel practices fair?" Do the selected words mean the same thing to everyone? What personnel? Which practices? Fair in what way?

To ensure that all respondents interpret the questions the same way, there are some general guidelines to follow. The team should use simple words. When a word exceeds seven letters, chances are that a shorter and more easily understood word can be substituted. Questions should not be too vague or too specific. The team must try to balance the general concept under investigation with the detailed information required. Close-ended questions with a few simple response choices may be appropriate for the specific data needed. The KISS principle, keeping it short and simple, should be kept in mind. The respondent is less likely to lose interest or misunderstand the question if questions are direct and concise.

Just as sampling quantitative items can be subject to bias, so can the collection of qualitative information. A biased question is one that influences people to respond in a manner that does not reflect accurately their positions on the issue under investigation. Slanting the wording of the question in one direction will not result in accurate information. The team should avoid the use of modifiers and qualifiers such as "help to," "may be," and words with strong emotional or persuasive appeal.

The team should not use hypothetical questions. These questions present situations that may not be realistic and ask respondents to suppose what they might do. This type of question can set up expectations, cause confusion, and misdirection, and is often of no real value to the survey. For example, the question "If you were transferred to a different section, where would you want to go?" might lead the respondent to think that such a change was actually about to occur.

Administering the survey begins the actual start of data collection. Successfully administering a survey requires careful preparation. The group must plan every detail of the process. Thorough preparation from the beginning will help the team avoid problems later.

The survey shown (Figure 4.3) is an example of a customer service survey developed by a quality improvement team. Note the variety of questions, the format, and the specific information requested.

Pareto Analysis

After the data have been collected it is analyzed by the team. One decision analysis tool used by groups is the Pareto chart. Decisions are often difficult to make, but the Pareto chart makes the process easier by visualizing collected data.

FIGURE 4.3

QUALITY OF CUSTOMER SERVICE SURVEY

1. I most frequently use the _____ office.
   (indicate location)
2. I do *most* of my banking business (check only one answer):
   ☐ with tellers in the lobby
   ☐ with people at the desks in the lobby
   ☐ with drive-up tellers
   ☐ with automated teller machines

3. When I go to the bank for service I usually have to wait:
   ☐ less than two minutes
   ☐ two to five minutes
   ☐ more than five minutes

   a. I find this amount of waiting time to be:
      ☐ reasonable and acceptable
      ☐ unacceptable

   b. I usually go to the bank on:
      ☐ Monday ☐ Tuesday ☐ Wednesday ☐ Thursday ☐ Friday ☐ Saturday

   c. I usually do my banking from:
      ☐ 9–11 AM ☐ 11 AM–1 PM ☐ 1–3 PM ☐ other _____

	ALMOST ALWAYS	USUALLY	INFREQUENTLY	ALMOST NEVER
4. My transactions are conducted in a timely manner				
5. When I visit the bank, my transactions are conducted in an error free manner				
6. My bank statements arrive on time				
7. My bank statements are free of errors				
8. When I visit the bank people: greet me with a smile				
call me by name				
are knowledgeable about my transactions				
thank me for my business				
9. When I call the bank on the telephone: the telephone is answered within three rings				
my questions are answered by the person answering the phone				
my call is transferred to someone else				
my telephone transactions are handled satisfactorily				
10. My bank office is well organized and maintained				
11. Bank people are neatly groomed				
12. Bank people treat me in a respectful manner				
13. I feel that my bank people care				
14. My bank is the financial institution I use most				
15. I recommend my bank to people I know				

FIGURE 4.3 (Continued)

16. If you ever had a problem with the bank, please describe its
    nature and approximate date.

    _____
    _____
    _____
    _____
    _____

    _____
17. If I could make one suggestion to my bank office it would be _____

    _____
    _____
    _____
    _____
    _____
    _____
    _____
    _____
    _____
    _____

In this way, comparisons can be made based on the facts. The Pareto chart clearly highlights the number one problem, and it does so with visual impact.

The Pareto Principle is a useful problem-solving technique that can save time and frustration by showing the team what problem to work on first. The diagram illustrates the problems that are wasting the most time, causing the most defects, or costing the most money. The major column identifies the problem the team should work on first. When that problem is solved, the next problem shown on the Pareto diagram (the second column) should be explored. By solving the most critical problem first, the team will be able to see the results almost immediately and receive recognition for a job well done.

The basic concept behind Pareto analysis is that when making decisions, the team wants to make the greatest improvement with the least time and effort. For example, the few important problems have greater potential for improvement than many trivial problems. Sometimes this concept is referred to as the ''80–20'' rule. For example, eighty percent of the office errors may be made by only twenty percent of the employees. The team follows several steps in constructing a Pareto chart.

- *Step 1*. Determine the time period in which data are to be collected. It may require hours, days, or even months.

- *Step 2*. Decide what information is to be gathered. Strategic choices at this time will ensure relevant, useful data.

- *Step 3*. Design a form that will allow the team to collect the data needed. This check sheet should be general enough so that the information can be arranged in a variety of ways.

- *Step 4*. Record the data on the check sheet.

- *Step 5*. Construct a Pareto chart that visually depicts the information on the check sheet. First, draw one horizontal line at the bottom of the page, and two vertical lines extending up from either side. Divide the horizontal line by the number of categories on the check sheet. The vertical line on

FIGURE 4.4

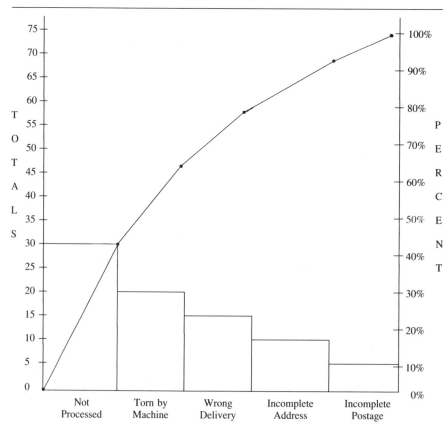

ERRORS

the left will be equal to the total amount of data collected. The line on the right will be equal to one hundred percent, since "total" means one hundred percent. The category with the largest number will be the bar on the far left. In Figure 4.4, the error categories are arranged as bars in descending order of the number of items collected. The result is a completed Pareto chart with the columns arranged in descending order, from left to right.

■ *Step 6*. Add a legend so others will know when the chart was constructed, which team constructed it, and what it depicts.

These Pareto charts (Figures 4.4 and 4.5) clearly highlight the number one problem and the most critical day for errors. The visual impact of the information is evident. The team can immediately see where to begin in solving the problem.

Teams should remember that occasionally a Pareto chart may contain a large number of columns. Often, the trivial columns are lumped together under one

FIGURE 4.5

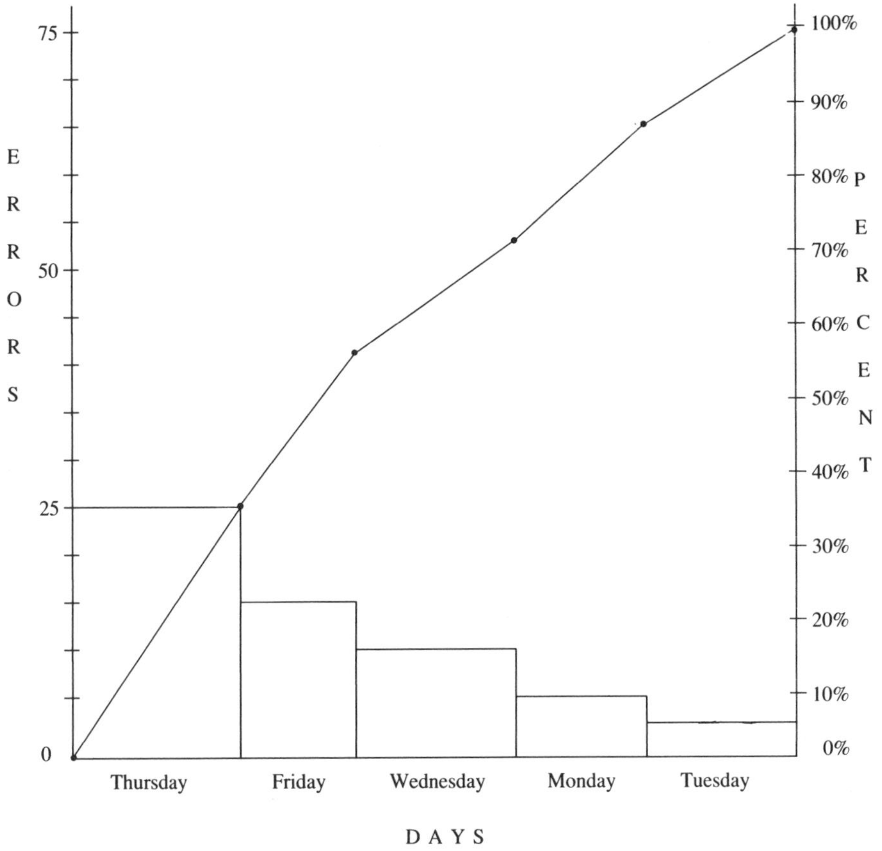

D A Y S

column entitled, "Other." The team should not ignore this small but important column.

After the team has identified the major problem with a Pareto chart, the number one problem is subjected to cause-and-effect analysis to find the true cause.

Cause-and-Effect Analysis

A *cause-and-effect diagram* is a picture composed of lines and symbols designed to represent a meaningful relationship between an effect and its possible causes. Teams use cause-and-effect diagrams to illustrate complex situations that are difficult to explain and analyze. For every effect, there are likely to be many interrelated causes. Cause-and-effect diagrams are designed to portray complex situations so that they can be better understood. This isolates the problem so that corrective action can be taken. Cause-and-effect diagrams are used to investigate either a "bad" effect to correct its causes, or a "good" effect to learn how to continue doing things efficiently.

The main purpose of this technique is to help the team solve problems in an organized and systematic manner. The problem is the "effect" and is written in the box to the right; the possible causes for the problem are written in the area to the left.

The following steps are used to construct a basic cause-and-effect diagram:

- ■ *Step 1*. State the problem or effect. The group should define the problem as precisely as possible. The members should not try to solve problems in other departments or areas outside their experience and control.

- ■ *Step 2*. Determine and identify the major cause groupings. Any number of such groupings is allowed. The four M's (materials, manpower, methods, and machines) are common and generally work well in helping the team establish possible causes. However, more experienced teams are likely to consider incorporating major groupings more specifically tailored to their needs.

- ■ *Step 3*. All team members participate in a brainstorming session. After the rules of brainstorming have been explained, the team can begin generating possible causes of the problem or effect.

Members should indicate the major grouping under which each of their individual ideas should be included. For example, a member might put "Negative Attitudes" under Manpower. The team is looking for causes, so members should try to state each idea as a specific cause, such as "Negative Attitude" instead of "Attitude."

During this brainstorming step, some team members tend to jump ahead and state solutions rather than possible causes. It is too early to assume that the true cause has been identified. In the problem of processing errors it would be premature to say, "develop new procedures." Team members should state a possible cause, such as, "Excessive Workload." The picture of the completed brainstorming session shows similar ideas grouped together in clusters that are simpler for the team to analyze.

- *Step 4.* The ideas collected during brainstorming are examined to identify those that are best. This is accomplished through a discussion and voting process. Identifying the best causes can be a time-consuming process involving a critical analysis of the pros and cons of each idea. The team can speed the process by giving members the opportunity to vote for each cause the members believe to be important. It may not seem scientific, but it works. Prior to voting, team members discuss any items that need further elaboration or clarification. At this time, similar ideas can be combined. By including this discussion step, time can be saved during the voting process.

- *Step 5.* The most probable causes are voted on again and ranked in order of importance. The team looks only at the items that receive the most votes. The pros and cons of each cause are discussed to gain further insight into the one most probable cause. The team recorder adds the priority ranking beside each of the major causes.

- *Step 6.* The most likely cause is tested in an attempt to verify it. This step may be simple or difficult and time-consuming, but it must always be done.

This is a simple cause-and-effect diagram (Figure 4.6) to determine possible causes of processing errors.

Work Simplification

Work simplification is a technique to make jobs more productive and meaningful by eliminating duplication and unnecessary tasks, or by recombining tasks to improve

FIGURE 4.6

Sample Cause-and-Effect Diagram

MATERIALS	MANPOWER
Disorganized records 4	Low motivation 7 4 #1
Missing items 3	Understaffed 6 1 #3

Processing Errors (effect)

METHODS	MACHINES
Lack of follow-up 5	
No monitoring procedure 7 2 #2	Machine malfunction 2
Excessive workload 6 0	

the effectiveness and efficiency of a particular flow process. The team uses a flow process work sheet to diagram the work process. Once the team has analyzed work processes, it can develop more efficient and productive work methods using work simplification techniques.

Before work simplification begins, an attitude (or determination) to improve efficiency must be present. A work simplification attitude means continuously looking for more effective and efficient ways of working. This process involves questioning the details of the job and looking for ways to improve it. Some questions the team might want to ask include: Why are we doing it this way? Are we doing it the best way? Is there a better way? By questioning all the details of a particular job, the team identifies opportunities for improvement in areas that at first glance may not appear to have problems. Once the group develops the right attitude, the next step in the work simplification concept is to understand work processes.

Work is the effort exerted to accomplish an objective. In general, work processes include three types of actions: (1) make-ready steps, (2) do steps, and (3) put-away steps. Only the do step is productive because it accomplishes the end result directly. However, employees perform a lot of nonproductive make-ready and put-away steps to get the do step done. Work simplification is a five-step process to find better and easier ways of getting work done.

■ *Step 1*. The team should select a problem. To aid in this process, the team needs to look at specific danger signals or symptoms that indicate that a problem exists.

Some examples of danger signals are listed in Table 4.3.

■ *Step 2*. After the team has selected a problem to work on, the next step is to document the details of the process. In doing this, a flow process work sheet can assist in gathering and organizing the information needed to solve the problem. The work sheet enables the group to give a step-by-step description of how the job is being done, the distances traveled, quantity or volume, and time information.

The initial step in documenting the details is to number and list on the work sheet every activity in a particular process in the order in which it occurs. The team should be as specific as possible when breaking down activities.

After listing the sequence of events, the next step is to classify each action or activity into one of five categories: (1) operations, (2) transportations, (3) inspections, (4) delays, and (5) storage.

○ *Operations* refer to steps in a process that help accomplish an objective. Usually, operation actions are the do step in a particular work process. However, not all of the operations are productive activities. Operation functions are always represented by a *circle*. Some examples of operation activities are typing a memorandum, stamping envelopes, or entering data into a computer.

→ *Transportations* refer to any action that requires physical movement from

TABLE 4.3

DANGER SIGNALS

Does the job involve:

Duplication? Is the same operation being performed by more than one person?

Deadlines? Are deadlines being met?

Delays? Is information for materials available?

Overtime? Is overtime frequent?

Bottlenecks? Are there situations where everything slows down?

Errors? Is error potential and conditions conducive to errors evident?

Roadblocks? Are there times when work cannot proceed?

Confusion? Are situations unclear or ill-defined?

Is the job:

Complicated? Could it be done more simply?

Fatiguing? Could it be done with less effort?

Tedious? Is the job tiresome and boring?

Time-consuming? Does the job take more time than results justify?

Does the job require:

Walking? Is too much time spent running around looking for files, materials, and people in other locations?

Searching? Is too much time spent searching for items and records that may be in their proper places, but too hard to find?

Backtracking? Is time spent going back over ground already covered?

Waiting? Is too much time spent waiting for information, reports, and materials to perform prerequisite actions?

Deciphering? Is too much time spent trying to read illegible or cryptic records?

© 1985, B. J. Chakiris Corporation. Reproduced with permission.

one place to another. Transportation actions are symbolized by an *arrow*. Although transportation activities are important, they are nonproductive activities.

☐ *Inspections* are those actions that involve some kind of checking, double checking, comparing, or proofreading. Inspection activities are represented by a *square*. Similar to transportation, inspection is also a nonproductive activity.

D *Delays* are symbolized by a half-moon shape that looks like the letter "D." Delay activities are the steps in a process where information or materials are not available for immediate access. Consequently, the work process slows down or stops temporarily. Examples of delays would be excessive system downtime, or waiting for report data. The team should include delays on the flow process work sheet as they are a danger signal that may indicate a problem exists.

▽ *Storage* usually involves filing or storing information for future use. Storage actions are identified by a *triangle*. Similar to transportation, inspection, and delays, storage functions are also nonproductive activities.

After the team has identified and categorized all actions into one of the five categories, members connect each action with the appropriate category on the work sheet. Once the team has connected all of the symbols, they have a clearer picture of the work process that will aid in analysis of the problem.

The team also records information such as distances traveled, quantity or volume, and time in the appropriate categories on the work sheet. Figure 4.7 is a completed flow process work sheet.

■ *Step 3.* When all the elements of a process have been documented, the team should discuss the details of each task to find more effective and efficient ways of doing the work. To accomplish this, the team has a brainstorming session or a general discussion to answer the following questions about each task:

What is this step? Why do we do it? Is it necessary?

Where are we doing it? Why there? Can we do it some other place?

When do we do it? Why at that time? Could we do it another time?

Who does it? Why? Can someone else do it?

How are we doing it? Why? Is there some other way to do it?

This may take substantial time and research, but the answers to these questions help the team develop alternative methods of doing the work. In general, there are only four ways to improve work processes: (1) eliminate, (2) combine, (3) change person, place, or sequence, or (4) improve the method. The various possibilities present themselves more readily if the group faithfully asks all the questions for each detail of the process. The team should record these possible alternatives on the flow process work sheet as well as on the brainstorming list for a permanent record and future reference.

■ *Step 4.* After listing possible alternatives or changes in task methods through questioning or brainstorming, the fourth step is to evaluate each possibility in terms of volume, quality, and time (VQT). The revised work process should produce the greatest volume of work, at an acceptable quality level, in the least amount of time. When these variables are added together, the result should be a reduction in costs.

Next, the team tests or verifies each new possibility against the VQT criteria and discards those that do not pass. This stage is mandatory. The group can either brainstorm to test the criteria or have an open discussion. Either way, it is important to make sure that the new alternative passes the VQT test.

Once the team verifies each possibility and eliminates those that do not pass, the remaining possibilities are combined into a new improved process that is smooth,

FIGURE 4.7

FLOW PROCESS WORK SHEET

PROCEDURE:	Chart Begins:	Chart Ends:	Charted By:	Date:
Quality Control Report	Volume Sheets Received	File Permanent Copy	Q. A. Analyst	

No.	Details of Procedure	OPER.	TRAN.	INSP.	DEL.	STOR.	DIST.	F INE T	QUAN.	TIME	ELIM.	COMB.	PER.	PLA.	SEQ.	IMPR.	Notes
1	Volume Sheets delivered	O	→	□	D	∇											
2	Stamp date received	O	→	□	D	∇											
3	Take work sheet to copy room	O	→	□	D	∇	500										
4	Make copy	O	→	□	D	∇			1								
5	Take copy back to desk	O	→	□	D	∇	500										
6	File old work sheet	O	→	□	D	∇	70										35 ft. each way
7	Enter and calculate percentages	O	→	□	D	∇				4 hr.							1 hr. enter 3 hr. calculate
8	File volume sheets	O	→	□	D	∇	70										
9	Take work sheet to word processing	O	→	□	D	∇	3,000										1,500 ft. each way
10	Wait for it to be typed	O	→	□	D	∇				3 hr.							Co-worker pick up Tuesday morning
11	Compare typing against original numbers	O	→	□	D	∇				½ hr.							Found error
12	Bring to word processing for correction	O	→	□	D	∇	3,000										
13	Pick up at word processing	O	→	□	D	∇	3,000										No mistakes
14	Calculate trend number	O	→	□	D	∇				1 hr.							
15	Give trends to "grapher" and wait	O	→	□	D	∇				5 day							Grapher can't get to graph
16	Write analysis	O	→	□	D	∇				½ hr.							
17	Bring to word processing	O	→	□	D	∇	3,000										Co-worker pick up Wednesday morning
18	Go to copy room and make copies of graph	O	→	□	D	∇	1,000		56	½ hr.							Long line
19	Go to copy room and make copies of analysis	O	→	□	D	∇	1,000		7								
20	Go to copy room and make reduced copies of rep.	O	→	□	D	∇	2,000		7	3 hr.							Reducer broken return later
21	Collate report and address envelopes	O	→	□	D	∇				15 min.							
22	Give to manager to review	O	→	□	D	∇				2 day							
23	Insert report in envelopes and put in out box	O	→	□	D	∇			7	15 min.							
24	File permanent copy	O	→	□	D	∇	70										
	TOTALS:	9	7	1	4	3	17,210		78	8 d 5 hr.							

productive, and efficient. The group should aim for thirty percent to fifty percent reduction in the number of steps.

■ *Step 5.* The final step is installing or implementing the new process. This step is the most important one because it represents the do step in the five-step pattern. This allows the group members to test their solution. The other four steps (selection of the problem, documentation, analysis, and design) are all make-ready steps that have no value unless the revised way is implemented and produces the expected improvements and savings.

When the team successfully implements the new process, it must monitor the results of the process to document the improvements.

After the team completes a project, the next step is to prepare a project benefit-and-cost analysis to document the process and results. This will be used to communicate project benefits when the project is presented to management for approval.

Cost Calculation and Project Benefits

As teams complete more projects, or membership within the group changes, the need to keep records of accomplishments becomes evident. Essentially, the group should keep track of what the projects were about, what actions were taken, and what the results were. One way of documenting team achievements is to complete a project benefit form and a cost calculation work sheet.

The cost calculation work sheet helps the team calculate the total dollar amount spent or saved as a result of resource increases or decreases from the project. The team should fill in the spaces with appropriate dollar amounts. In addition to the money saved or spent as a result of the project recommendation, there are a number of one-time costs to be included. These costs relate specifically to things such as time spent or purchases made during the course of the project.

In completing the form, the team should record important demographic information such as work unit and team name. The team should also list names of the facilitator, leader, and all team members, as well as anyone from outside the group who provided assistance on the project. This first section of the form includes the start date and completion date for the project. The group should also indicate how many hourly meetings were required to complete the project. Any meetings that were cancelled should be omitted and extra sessions for "dry runs" and special activities should be included.

An important section of the form is documentation of the project's purpose and what was involved. The group describes the focus of the project and how the team selected the project. The various techniques used to analyze the topic, including problem-solving techniques such as brainstorming, Pareto, and cause-and-effect analyses should be listed. The team also details the research it did to collect information and numerical data, and the format of this information.

The team should include pertinent information regarding team procedures and analysis of the facts, selected causes, verification techniques and outcomes, and any outside assistance received (e.g., from other teams, staff personnel, section employees, or management). This information must be checked for accuracy and logic.

The final recommendation is described next. The team explains the best solution to the problem and makes recommendations for improvements. This section is supported by the information the team has already provided on the form.

Results are perhaps the most important part of the benefits analysis. The team also should provide a description of project benefits that may be more difficult to measure. For example, did morale or attitudes improve as a result of the project? Do team members have a better understanding of procedures or the work unit? Are employees communicating more effectively with each other and management? What did the team gain, as individuals or as a group, from completing this project?

The manager should decide on which of these areas of improvement the accepted recommendation impacted the most: quality, productivity, customer service, or the work area. The improvements should be expressed numerically. If not, the group can suggest ways to measure the results. The group then completes the cost analysis calculation by indicating the overall cost or savings derived from the team project.

This project information and the cost analysis calculation are excellent ways to document team achievements. The completed project information and cost analysis can also be used to publicize team achievements. The team should send copies to managers and to the coordinator and department facilitator. If the division or department has a newsletter, the completed form can be used as an outline for an article about the team recommendation and presentation. This may also help the team organize its presentation and verify that the facts and analysis support the proposal.

The benefits that are realized if the recommendation is accepted can help the team sell its ideas to management at the presentation. It is impressive when the team illustrates expected results with projected savings and benefit measurements.

The Project Benefits summary sheet (Figure 4.8) and the Cost Calculation Work Sheet (Figure 4.9) are included on the next several pages.

Management Presentation

After completing the forms, the team is ready to prepare for the management presentation. The presentation, formal or informal, is given by the leader and team members. The facilitator is usually present. The presentation is important because management is informed of team activities and accomplishments, and team members are recognized for their contributions. Management response to the presentation is equally important. An estimated ninety percent of team recommendations are accepted and implemented in most companies. However, if a manager does not accept a proposal, it is essential that the manager explain the reasons for the rejection, and show support and enthusiasm for the team's efforts.

Once a decision on a proposal is made by a manager, the team can either select a new problem to work on or revise the former proposal if it was not accepted. Although the facilitator is now spending less time with the group, the quality of group interaction should remain high. The facilitator can assist the team in revising a rejected recommendation, finding a new direction, or lending moral support when an idea is rejected. Management presentations should be made

FIGURE 4.8

PROJECT BENEFITS
Project Summary

I. *General Information*

Division Name _____ Section Name _____

Team Name _____ Facilitator _____

Leader _____

Members _____

_____ _____

_____ _____

_____ _____

_____ _____

Special Assistance _____

Project Start Date _____ Project Completion Date _____

Number of Meetings to Complete Project ___

II. *Project Documentation*

Project Name or Theme _____

Purpose _____

_____

Problem Selection/Solving Techniques Used:

      Technique   *Use*

Analysis of Information Collected _____

_____

_____

Recommendation _____

_____

III. *Management Presentation*

Date ___/___/___

Presented to: _____ _____

Accepted or Rejected (Circle One) Date ___/___/___

Explanation _____

_____

Modifications of Proposal _____

_____

Special Presentation Techniques Used: _____

- -

Date ___/___/___

Presented to: _____ _____

Accepted or Rejected (Circle One) Date ___/___/___

Explanation _____

_____

Modifications of Proposal _____

_____

Special Presentation Techniques Used: _____

FIGURE 4.8 (Continued)

IV. *Results*
Benefits Description _____

The accepted recommendation impacts which area the *most?* (Have your manager select *one;* note measurable results or comments.)

   Area   *Measurements, Comments*

Quality (prevented/reduced errors) _____
Productivity (reduced manhours/resources/costs) _____
Work Area (environment more conducive to work/safety) _____
Customer Service (enhanced services or understanding of job) _____
Implementation Date ____/____/____
Additional Information _____

Overall Cost or Savings (Circle One) of Project in Year 1: $_____
   (line E on Cost Calculation Worksheet)
Overall Cost or Savings (Circle One) of Project in year 2 and beyond: $_____
   (line C on Cost Calculation Worksheet)

every three months or so. Sometimes more than one project can be covered during a single presentation. The presentation should not surprise the manager by putting the manager on the spot with unexpected requests for solutions, funding, or manpower increases. The manager must be kept informed of the team's activities on a regular basis. This can be done by sending copies of the minutes of the meetings and discussing the group's progress informally on a periodic basis.

Team members are introduced at the beginning of the presentation. As many team members as possible should be involved as speakers. Each should be introduced immediately before speaking, either by the chairperson or the preceding speaker. The team may use charts that illustrate the techniques it has mastered, such as Pareto and cause-and-effect analysis. This helps to get the message across quickly and makes a good impression. The team should use the same charts that were prepared during the team meeting rather than redoing them. This is easier and adds a note of realism.

The milestone chart is an effective way to show how the team has scheduled and monitored its activities. Line graphs are popular because of the ease with which they can be constructed. Pie charts and bar charts are also familiar tools.

There are other methods besides the more commonly used visual aids that can help get the team message across. For example, if the members have revised some forms, they can bring some copies of the old forms and the revised versions to the presentation. The manager should see the actual results of teamwork firsthand, if possible. If necessary, the team can have everyone adjourn to the work area to witness the changes, or proposed changes. Handouts can also be helpful. However, if they are distributed too early, the audience may pay more attention to the material than the speakers in the team presentation.

FIGURE 4.9

Cost Calculation Work Sheet

Introduction

Individual employees and problem-solving teams know intuitively when they are working more effectively; volume increases, errors decrease, time required to process items drops, customers are more satisfied and morale improves. Unfortunately, the ease with which individuals quantify these benefits varies. The purpose of this work sheet is to assist you in justifying actual or proposed changes in your work area and in documenting the improvements which have been made.

Instructions

Sections III and IV include a number of questions that can be used for evaluating the cost effectiveness of your recommendation. Answer each question, in a dollar amount, if it applies to your recommendation. If the question doesn't apply to your project, simply add in a zero, "0." Total the dollar amounts for each line in sections I, II and III as you complete them. Section IV provides information that enables you to calculate the actual dollar savings.

I. *Labor, Equipment, Area, Materials or Procedures Decreased*   *Dollar Amount*

   A. *Labor*

   Did you eliminate the staff required to complete a task or an operation (FTE × midpoint of grade level previously doing job (function)? $ _____

   Will new equipment reduce the amount of time required to process an item [(original # hours required to process one item − # hours required with new equipment) × annual volume of item × hourly salary midpoint of personnel performing operation]?   _____

   Will changes in floor plan improve work flow [(# hours required to process item with old plan − # hours required to process item with new plan) × annual volume of item × hourly salary midpoint of personnel performing operation)]?   _____

   Will elimination/revision of materials used decrease the time required to complete work [(original # hours required to complete daily work − # hours required with elimination of materials) × # work days per year × hourly salary midpoint of personnel completing work]?   _____

   Was the time required to complete the task or operation reduced as a result of procedural changes [(original # hours required to complete the task − revised # hours) × # times task performed per year × hourly salary midpoint of personnel performing operation]?   _____

   B. *Equipment*

   Did you eliminate the need for any equipment originally costing over $200.00* (annual depreciation = original cost of the equipment + 5 years)?   _____

   C. *Area*

   Will changes in floor plan reduce space needed by the division (square footage saved × monthly occupancy fee per square foot × 12 months)?   _____

   D. *Materials*

   Was supplies usage eliminated or reduced (# items eliminated per year × cost of that item)?   _____

   E. *Procedures*

   Were procedures changed that eliminated or reduced the internal or external service fees previously charged (e.g., microfilming, storage, systems)? (Eliminated = monthly fee × 12 months) [Reduced = (old monthly fee − new monthly fee) × 12 months]   _____

   SECTION I SUBTOTAL $ _____

   * If equipment is 6 years old or older or original cost is less than $200.00, there is no cost savings.

FIGURE 4.9 (Continued)

II. *Labor, Equipment, Areas, Materials or Procedures Increased*   *Dollar Amount*

   A. *Labor*

   Did you increase the staff required to do the job (FTE × midpoint of salary grade level doing the job)? $ _____

   Will equipment increase the amount of time required to process an item [(# hours required to process one item with new equipment − original # hours required) × annual volume of item × hourly salary midpoint of personnel performing operation]?   _____

   Will proposed changes in floor plan delay work flow [(# hours required to process items with new plan − original # or hours required to process items) × annual volume of item × # hourly salary midpoint of personnel performing operation)]?   _____

   Will additional materials increase the time required to prepare/process work [(# hours required to complete daily work with additional materials − original # hours) × # work days per year × hourly salary midpoint of personnel completing work]?   _____

   Was the time required to complete the task or operation increased as a result of procedural changes [(# hours with revised procedures to complete the task − original # hours) × # times task performed per year × hourly salary midpoint of personnel performing operation]?   _____

   B. *Equipment*

   Was equipment over $200.00 purchased (annual depreciation cost = purchase price + 5 years)?   _____

   * See Section III, B for related one-time costs.

   C. *Area*

   Was additional divisional space for storage or work flow acquired (square footage acquired × monthly occupancy fee per square foot × 12 months)?   _____

   D. *Material*

   Were additional supplies acquired (# items added per year × cost of that item)?   _____

   E. *Procedures*

   Were procedures changed which added or increased internal or external service fees charged (e.g., microfilming, storage, systems)? (Added = monthly fee × 12 months) [Increased = (new monthly fee − old monthly fee) × 12 months]

   SECTION II SUBTOTAL $ _____

III. *One-Time Project Costs*

   A. *Labor*

   What labor costs are associated with your project [(# hourly meetings × # members × average hourly midpoint of members) + (# hourly meetings attended by facilitator or advisor × hourly midpoint of facilitator or advisor)]? $ _____

   What is the cost of resources used during project (e.g., systems consultation, stationery or forms design, start-up training costs, etc.)? (Consultation costs = # hours consultation × hourly salary midpoint of consultant and trainees)   _____

   B. *Equipment*

   Were purchase-related fees charged for purchases of equipment over $200.00 (e.g., installation fees, service contract fees, etc.)?   _____

   Were additional costs incurred through the modification/repair of equipment (e.g., parts price, repair costs, service fees)?   _____

   Was equipment $200.00 or under purchased (e.g., purchase price and installation fees, etc.)?   _____

   C. *Area*

   Were any area construction costs incurred for the project? (Project cost)   _____

   SECTION III SUBTOTAL $ _____

FIGURE 4.9 (Continued)

IV. *Cost/Savings Difference*

What is the subtotal of Section I (estimated savings)?	A. _____
What is the subtotal of Section II (estimated costs)?	B. _____
What is the difference between the two subtotals (Line A − Line B = overall savings from year two and beyond)?	C.$ _____
What is the subtotal of Section III (one-time costs)?	D. _____
What is the difference between lines C and D (Line C − Line D = net savings for first year)?	E.$ _____

The value of Line C indicates actual overall savings (or costs) for your recommendation from the second year and beyond. If the amount is positive, it indicates an overall savings (e.g., C = 5,000 represents savings of $5,000). If the amount is negative, it indicates the overall cost (e.g., C = −6,000 means costs of $6,000).

The amount on Line D represents the start-up costs which are incurred only during your project and for the first year that your recommendation is implemented.

Line E's value indicates net savings (or costs) for the first year of your recommendation's implementation.

V. *Notes and Calculations*

The management presentation is one of the greatest rewards for team members. They explain the problem they have identified, the techniques they have used to analyze the problem, and the solution they have developed to solve the problem. Table 4.4 is a typical agenda for a management presentation.

Recognition and Reward

The management presentation is the best opportunity for management to recognize team activities with supportive comments and helpful suggestions. Team management presentations to high level management or other departments and companies provide the group with a unique and special form of recognition. Public recognition

TABLE 4.4

Agenda for Management Presentation

Welcome and Introductions	Leader
Project Overview	Member One
Problem Identification	Member Two
Problem Analysis	Member Three
Implementation of Solution	Member Four
Benefits and Savings to Organization	Member Five
Preview of Upcoming Project	Member Six
Concluding Remarks	Leader
Questions and Answers	

through professional societies such as the American Society for Quality Control and the International Association of Quality Circles, or journals such as *Quality Progress* and *Quality Magazine,* as well as various internal newspapers or newsletters, quarterly reports, office bulletins, and division meetings can also be effective motivators. Publication of team progress in external publications adds prestige and esteem to group efforts.

The performance appraisal and salary administration systems, although not used directly to reward team involvement, can reflect an employee's personal growth and contribution through participation in a quality team. However, this can be difficult and in some cases impossible to measure in an accurate way. Material

TABLE 4.5

QUALITY TEAMS
Project Reward Example

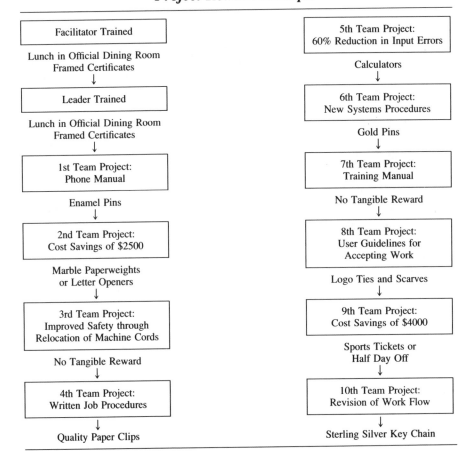

Facilitator Trained	**5th Team Project:** 60% Reduction in Input Errors
Lunch in Official Dining Room Framed Certificates ↓	Calculators ↓
Leader Trained	**6th Team Project:** New Systems Procedures
Lunch in Official Dining Room Framed Certificates ↓	Gold Pins ↓
1st Team Project: Phone Manual	**7th Team Project:** Training Manual
Enamel Pins ↓	No Tangible Reward ↓
2nd Team Project: Cost Savings of $2500	**8th Team Project:** User Guidelines for Accepting Work
Marble Paperweights or Letter Openers ↓	Logo Ties and Scarves ↓
3rd Team Project: Improved Safety through Relocation of Machine Cords	**9th Team Project:** Cost Savings of $4000
No Tangible Reward ↓	Sports Tickets or Half Day Off ↓
4th Team Project: Written Job Procedures	**10th Team Project:** Revision of Work Flow
↓ Quality Paper Clips	↓ Sterling Silver Key Chain

rewards, such as certificates or pins, are used most often to remind members that their contributions to the organization are appreciated.

The concept of ''gainsharing'' or sharing the cost savings or revenue enhancement with the team members is a popular and effective motivator. This may be done directly by awarding a percentage of the savings or revenue to the members or by directly awarding a predetermined amount to the work group based upon a period of increased productivity, quality, volume, sales, or other measurable factor that should improve as a result of team projects being completed. This latter method is similar to a Scanlon Plan. A more diluted and less direct method is profit sharing or the currently popular 401(k) plans. These reward everyone for better performance and less directly reward or motivate the individual team members.

Management should always share the gains with team members—employees. Whether it be only through merit increases or percent savings, it is the fair and long-term motivator.

The recognition given to quality team activities can be the single most significant factor for sustaining momentum and enthusiasm in members. Therefore, the ways in which the group is recognized are important considerations for the steering committee or advisory group. An example of a reward cycle is shown in Table 4.5.

This chapter has given a detailed analysis of quality improvement teams in action in a traditional organizational structure with primary focus on the use of specific problem-solving techniques in gathering, analyzing, and presenting information. Training teams in these techniques is absolutely necessary for their success.

Evaluation of results in relation to organizational goals is critical in maintaining management support of participation and employee involvement. Methods of measuring results are the focus of Chapter 5.

Acknowledgment

Portions of the preceding material on planning, flow charting, sampling, survey data collection, work simplification, and cost calculation and benefit analysis are taken from *Employee Involvement in Quality and Productivity,* a media-supported training program, developed and distributed by B. J. Chakiris Corporation, Chicago. This material is used by permission of B. J. Chakiris Corporation.

CHAPTER 5
Measuring the Results of Employee Involvement

Objective and Subjective Data

Measuring the results of employee involvement activities is essential. Only scientifically and methodically gathered data will serve as evidence of success and appease skeptical critics. Measurement data also provide feedback for teams to support changes and stimulate improvement. Both objective and subjective data can assist companies in evaluating the quality team process.

There are many ways to track group effectiveness using objective information. Quality measures and standards programs can be implemented simultaneously, or preferably, prior to team initiation. These programs provide the necessary performance indices and defect rates to compare performances before and after implementing quality teams.

Tangible results can also be viewed from a financial perspective. Companies can easily determine their return on investment by monitoring savings as a result of team operation, compared to costs involved in the implementation and operation of the teams. Payback ratios in companies where quality teams have been implemented successfully range from two to one to eight to one.

Productivity, absenteeism, turnover, disciplinary orders, firings, hirings from within company ranks, and use of medical and counseling services are all variables that can be quantified and monitored, before and after implementation, and used as indicators of the success of the process.

Records of team activities should be maintained carefully. These records provide case studies of what has been accomplished and how much was saved. They also serve as a foundation for team reports to senior level company officials. These reports can assimilate the recorded information for detailed analysis of the success or failure of the process.

Objective data for rating team activities are sometimes hard to obtain and, because of the qualitative nature of these activities, subjective measurement is equally necessary to determine the success of the involvement process. Howard Ferguson, manager of quality circles for the Westinghouse Defense and Electronics Systems Center, stated, "The intangible results of increased employee job satisfaction, improved employee-management communication . . . are immeasurable objectively, but I feel the return is even greater than for tangible matters."

These intangible results can be measured through employee displays of increased quality consciousness, improved morale and communications, and increased interest in and attendance at team meetings. Perhaps the most empirical way of capturing these subjective data is by conducting attitude surveys. Asking direct questions of employees, managers, and team members can give added insight into the effectiveness and impact of quality teams.

The importance of these attitudes was expressed by C. H. Molde, an operations vice president for one corporation, ". . . we don't just measure our success in terms of dollars saved or circles in operation. More important factors to us are the way our working style has changed and the way productivity and quality of working life have improved in our division."

Other subjective measures, for example, recognition and feedback from outside sources such as customer complaints and customer perception surveys, can be monitored to help evaluate team operations, progress, or methods. The articles and presentations about the participative process within an organization that are accepted or requested by outside publications or organizations also provide recognition for that organization.

Measurement of changes that occur directly and indirectly, planned or unplanned, from employee involvement and participation activities is vital. Not measuring or inadequately measuring results is probably the main reason why most teams fail or give only minimal results. Failure is most often linked to management support. Whether the stated excuse for failure is "poor leaders," "ran out of problems," or "lack of member interest," lack of management support is usually the real cause. Any problem can be solved if management wants it solved. However, without some proof of tangible results, management will not offer continued support.

Lack of management support can be present initially even though management gives the go-ahead to start a participative program. This attitude can continue and become more negative, or it can change and become truly supportive. In some cases, an initially supportive management can become unsupportive if it does not see proven benefits and bottom-line results.

The key to management support is empirical evidence of tangible and intangible results or improvements. Empirical evidence cannot be provided unless measurements are made. Not measuring or ineffective measuring will inevitably lead to a lack of adequate management support whether that support was present initially or not. Once the program is "sold" to management and started, a significant hurdle is past. Beginning the process requires relatively progressive management that believes in participative concepts. Yet no matter how progressive management may be, measurement is the continuing foundation for true ongoing management support that sustains the employee involvement process.

Process Measurement

Measurement is also important in effectively administering and managing the participative process. Process measures can help evaluate the process itself to ensure that it is functioning correctly and running smoothly.

The first process measure is to keep a record of those people who were given an opportunity to participate, when they were trained, and whether or not they chose to be a part of a team after the initial orientation or training. These records should be kept continuously. When people decide to drop out of the process or when employees who decided initially not to be a part of the process later decide to become team members, the records should reflect this activity. These records will help identify and determine the average membership length, how long people are involved in the team, and the ratio of new members joining to other members leaving the process.

The date that the teams are established and begin to function and the date that the teams cease to function should be noted. These records determine the average life of a team. This will also help establish the ratio of new teams to old teams.

Keeping records on the amount of time individuals are involved in the process and which teams are functioning the longest will help identify the health of the involvement process and assess which characteristics are causing the members to be sustained in the process longer. Teams that only last for a short period also can be analyzed and exit interviews can be given to members who are leaving the process. It is important that the process be monitored. For example, if the organization sustains a level of one hundred employees in the process but is continuously training new participants to replace lost team members, there is a serious problem that should be addressed. This same analysis holds true with teams, if new teams are added at an equivalent rate to replace old teams that are dropped or retired. The ratio of new teams to retired should be no lower than twenty to one. Dropping below this number means there is a problem in the process or organization. The ratio of new team members to retired will initially be eight to one, but as the process matures this will rise to fifteen to one or greater.

The number of projects underway and the time span from the beginning to the end of a project also should be recorded. It is important to determine how long it takes on the average to complete projects. The coordinator can keep an eye on those projects that tend to be much longer than the average project to determine whether intervention needs to be made to speed the project, to make sure that it is on track, or to lend assistance to the members in wrapping it up. In some cases the project may be long and involved and needs to run longer. If the organization is not tracking project length, it may lose a number of groups because teams lose direction and a sense of accomplishment.

Support resources can be spread throughout the system by keeping a record of where the teams are located within the organization. Individual departments should be contacted to determine if they are interested in the participative process. If all teams and resources are in a single area, it could cause morale problems in other areas because people may believe that they are being avoided for some reason. It is better to spread the resources equally throughout five departments and begin five teams in five different departments rather than to start five teams in a single department.

The participation rate should also be calculated. There are several methods that can be used. The first method is to calculate the number of members who join the teams after being trained as a percentage of the total number of employees trained (fifty percent to ninety percent is normal). Another way to look at participation rate is to look at the number of employees trained as a percentage of the total employees in the area. A third way is to look at the total number of employees who decide to be on a team after being trained as a percentage of the total number of people in the area. These last two ratios vary greatly depending on the stage of the program. All of these measures are easily calculated and are helpful in diagnosing the health of the participative process as it develops. These data can also help pinpoint areas that may have major problems in the future. In the early stages, difficulties can be diagnosed and addressed while they are still minor problems.

For all of the process measures discussed, there is no right answer as to what each individual measure should be for a particular organization or industry, or for involvement teams in general. There are some trends in similar industries

TABLE 5.1

Measures of Effectiveness

Leaders Trained	All supervisors who have had training during the current month or quarter.
Inactive Teams	Teams who were trained but had all volunteers drop out after the team started.
Number Teams	The number of teams meeting on a regular basis.
Number Potential Volunteers	Personnel who have received orientation and have had the opportunity to join a team, i.e., full-time employees plus the part-time employees who work at the time the teams are scheduled to meet.
Number Actual Volunteers	Current number of members in the team, excluding the leaders.
Percent Volunteers	Actual volunteers ÷ potential volunteers.
Number Projects Started	Total number of projects started this month.
Number Projects Completed/Approved	Projects that have been presented to the level of management necessary to give final approval.
Number Projects Completed/Rejected	Projects that have been presented to the level of management that has the last word on rejection.
Number Projects Dropped	Those projects started, i.e., data collected, etc., but discontinued prior to management presentation.
Improved Work Quality	Number of projects that improved turnaround time or prevented errors or defects.
Improved Production	Number of projects that improved processing time or reduced cost.
Improved Work Area	Number of projects that made the physical environment more conducive to work and safety.
Improved Service	Number of projects that enhanced products or services.
Net Annual Savings	All the costs of the current operations or process (the way we are doing things) less all the costs of the proposed operations or process (the way we recommend doing things). This includes implementation costs (if any) but does not include project time or resources to develop the proposal, although this time will be tracked and recorded.

that may be helpful. However, each program will be unique, and, the overall coordinator should simply keep track of the numbers and compare the numbers with progression for each area. The aggregate will indicate what works and what does not work for that organization.

Tables 5.1, 5.2, 5.3, and 5.4 illustrate some of the definitions of effectiveness measures, basic formulas, and sample results.

TABLE 5.2

Volunteer Rate and Participation Rate

O r i e n t a t i o n T r a i n i n g P r o j e c t	A	Number of potential members (in orientation meeting)	+
	B	Number of personnel changes in first thru fourth meeting	±
	C	Number of potential partici-pants (A ± B)	sub tl
	D	Number of potential partici-pants chose not to join before fifth meeting	−
	E	Number of volunteers (C − D)	sub tl
	F	Number of volunteers who dropped fifth meeting thru end of training	−
	G	Number of personnel changes fifth meeting thru end of train-ing	±
	H	Number of participants who trained or are in training (E − F ± G)	TL
	I	Number of participants who dropped after training	−
	J	Number of personnel changes	±
	K	Number of participants who decided to rejoin	+
	L	Number of active members (H − I ± J + K)	TL

$$\text{Volunteer Rate} = \frac{E}{C} \times 100\%$$

$$\text{Participation Rate} = \frac{L}{C} \times 100\%$$

TABLE 5.3

Team Statistics
Year End

Dept.	Teams	Members	Participation Rate
Bond	4	29	59%
Charge Card	9	71	76%
Chk. Proc.	38	239	49%
Controllers	7	45	73%
Dist. Svcs.	2	13	65%
GBS Ops.	81	535	59%
Mgmt. Svcs.	4	32	100%
Personnel	2	16	84%
Systems	2	18	100%
Current Year Totals:	149	998	59%
Previous Year Totals:	117	840	57%

TABLE 5.4

Orientation/Volunteer Rate

Area	Teams	Participation Rate (%)	Volunteers Total Staff (Members)	Potential/ Total Staff (Oriented)
Bond	4	59%	28%	48%
Charge Card	9	76%	54%	70%
Check Processing	38	49%	15%	30%
Controllers	7	73%	43%	59%
GBS Operations	81	59%	38%	65%
Totals:	139	58%	27%	48%

Results Measurement

The next set of measures relates to the results or the effectiveness of employee involvement and the direct tangible benefits that are derived from the participative process.

It is important to understand that the tangible benefits can also be strong motivators. The team members, as they review the results of the measures, can see directly how their activities are contributing to the improvement of their company, their work area, and their team. As a result, employees know that they personally have contributed to this integrated effort.

After the team has brainstormed and selected a project or issue to work on, this project should be added to an ongoing list of all the current problems or issues of all of the teams. There are many benefits in maintaining this comprehensive list. For example, two teams may be working on similar projects that complement each other. In this case, the teams may work together, possibly sharing techniques, approaches, and even data. Additionally, by reviewing the projects, management can make sure that there are not individual projects being developed by management that may be identical to those being investigated by the teams. It can be disastrous for a team to work on a project for several months only to find that when it makes a recommendation to management, management has been working on the same problem and may already have a solution. Management may also find that there are inappropriate projects being developed by the team. If this is identified early in the project, the team can be approached to change or modify the project and a discussion can take place as to why that project may be inappropriate.

The date the project was started should also be recorded along with the name of the project being pursued. This will allow an easy review to determine whether projects are running inordinately long, and if they are, if some type of intervention or help may be needed to complete the project. Average project time should run between three and six months. The first projects will run longer because the team members are learning the techniques by applying them. It is important that the initial project or projects be limited in scope and complexity. This allows the team members to concentrate specifically on learning the methods they are using to attack the problem. If a problem is too difficult or complex, the group may not be able to get a firm grasp of the techniques because of the overwhelming problem. If projects begin to run over six months, it is important that intervention take place. The team should be consulted to find out if there is a difficulty with the project or if it is close to completion. In some cases the team may be making good progress, but simply needs more time.

In case of extremely long projects—projects that are going to take over six months—it is a good idea to make the progress report presentation to management sometime in the interim. This will give team members a sense of accomplishment as they proceed with the project and will force them into summarizing results to date. The team may also be motivated by management's positive response to its efforts.

The list of current projects should be distributed to the teams for their review and should also be distributed to all managers in the organization (Figure 5.1).

Another helpful and necessary measurement is to keep track of the completed projects. This can be done easily and is an excellent tool for managers to review quickly what has been accomplished and the tangible results. The information recorded should include the name of the issue or problem being worked on, the start date, and the calendar weeks or months needed to complete the project. In addition, the total number of hours the project consumed should be recorded. The results of the project must be summarized. This can be done simply by developing categories in which projects can be assigned. An excellent approach would include the following categories:

■ Measurable Quality Improvement (reduced errors, defects, or complaints)

■ Measurable Productivity Improvement (reduced resource usage or cost)

FIGURE 5.1

Check Processing—Quality Teams
Project Status Report

Open Projects

Project Title or description	Division	Section	Team Name	Start Date	Estimated Completion Date
Automation of manual logging system	Balance Control	Investigators	Target Seven		
Possibility of sectional restructuring to enhance control of correspondence	Balance Control	Supervisors	Super Circle		
Lack of knowledge and functions of Balance Control Responsibilities	Balance Control	Cash Back	Error Traffic Controllers		
Cross training	Demand Deposit	Receipt of Reports	Third World		
Bad ID of tapes received from customer	Demand Deposit	Account Reconcilement	The Problem Solvers		
Training program on subject of availability	Document Processing Center	Machine Room Day Force	The Minority Majority		
Converting from paper to fiche for balancing purposes	Document Processing Center	Cashiers Checks	Trouble-Shooters		

■ Measurable Service Improvement (new, improved, or modified products or services)

■ Improvement in the Work Environment (work area changes to improve the quality of work life or safety)

Placing all projects into these categories shows at a glance what kinds of projects are being pursued by the teams. As the teams review this report these four types of project categories will appear to be objectives of the kinds of projects that management is encouraging. Not only can this be a measure, but it can also give the teams an idea of the direction the company wants them to go with their projects.

A summary of the actual benefits accrued by the completion of the investigation or project should also be included. This can be simply one or two sentences describing the benefits of implementing the solution. In this summary an individual project may fall into more than one of the previously mentioned categories. In that case, a decision must be made as to which category is affected the most and the project is then assigned to that particular category. If there are any cost savings or revenue increases projected to be achieved through the project, the net of these should also be indicated on the project summary. An analysis sheet for documenting and calculating the cost savings or revenue generation of a project is included in Chapter 4.

It is also helpful on this particular measurement report to record whether the project was accepted or rejected, and if it was rejected, why? If it is accepted, the reward and recognition given to the team members for their efforts should also be recorded. This indication of reward or recognition can give other managers new ideas on how they can reward and recognize their own people.

Tables 5.5, 5.6, 5.7, and 5.8 document completed projects and results measurement in the four categories.

Performance Measurement

Performance measures are also tangible measurements of the results that take place in the work area from the participation process. In many cases, there will be other influences in the work area that could cause changes in these measures. These definitely are tangible and may be classified as direct measures only if there is a stable environment where the only change and new process is the involvement teams. If there are other new major influences in the work area, the use of these production measures should be considered indirect. It is important that these performance measures are established before the actual implementation of the process.

Measurable Quality Improvement

The first performance measure is *quality measurement.* Quality measures are usually made up of simple ratios, for example, the number of typing errors over the number of lines or pages typed. It is important to develop a quality measure for each major change of state taking place in the work process to determine what the quality is for each of the major steps in the process. These quality measures are not necessarily set on each individual. Obviously, if only one person is performing a particular step then that measure would reflect the individual's performance, but where there are many people performing a particular step this would be a group performance measure, rather than an individual measure. These measures should be established before implementation of employee involvement. It is not unusual to have a ratio of one or two measures per employee in an area.

Table 5.9 illustrates performance measures in a quality monitoring system.

Measurable Productivity Improvement

Another method of performance measurement is *productivity measures.* Productivity measurement involves a simple ratio for the group of the number of

TABLE 5.5

Completed Projects

DIVISION— Document Processing   SECTION—Reconcilement Controls/Night Force
TEAM NAME—Pathfinder
PROJECT— Missing HSRR Totals
SOLUTION— Put all HSRR strings in a different color binder; identify with date, cycle and shift; Number the filing system by cycle
BENEFITS— Central location of computer-generated reports; reduce person hours in balancing which will reduce cost
NUMBER OF HOURS TO COMPLETE—34[*]

DIVISION— Balance Control   SECTION—Supervisors   TEAM NAME—Super Circle
PROJECT— Feasibility of sectional restructuring to enhance control to correspondence
SOLUTION— Restructuring of correspondence files; revised letter follow-up system; established method of following-up phone calls
BENEFITS— Improve turnaround answering correspondence; faster resolution of differences; elimination of unnecessary correspondence; expedite preparation for difference resolution meetings
NUMBER OF HOURS TO COMPLETE—100

DIVISION— Balance Control   SECTION—Investigators   TEAM NAME—Target 7
PROJECT— Eliminate manual investigation logging
SOLUTION— Modifications to D.M.S. system
BENEFITS— Reduce overtime; improve turnaround time
NUMBER OF HOURS TO COMPLETE—30

DIVISION— Demand Deposit Services   SECTION—Retail Check Paying
TEAM NAME—Super Solvers
PROJECT— Training guide
SOLUTION— Supplement to procedures and glossary of commonly used terms
BENEFITS— Improved training orientation
NUMBER OF HOURS TO COMPLETE—74

DIVISION— Document Processing   SECTION—Machine Room/Evening Force
TEAM NAME—Speedballs
PROJECT— Maintenance cabinet with material for each sorter
SOLUTION— A tray for each individual sorter containing materials for maintaining 3890 sorters
BENEFITS— Reduced rejects 0.4%; responsibility for maintaining equipment; better maintenance; $25,458 cost savings
NUMBERS OF HOURS TO COMPLETE—20

DIVISION— Demand Deposit Services   SECTION—Receipt of Reports
TEAM NAME—Third World
PROJECT— Cross-Training
SOLUTION— All section members cross-trained on machine-related jobs
BENEFITS— Increased flexibility in work assignments
NUMBER OF HOURS TO COMPLETE—86

DIVISION— Demand Deposit Services   SECTION—Check Register
TEAM NAME—Trouble Shooters
PROJECT— Converting paper reports to fiche for daily balancing
SOLUTION— Procedures revised and conversion arranged
BENEFITS— $30,000 reduction in systems operations expenses
NUMBER OF HOURS TO COMPLETE—110

DIVISION— Demand Deposit Services   SECTION—ARS Reconcilement
TEAM NAME—ARS Problem Solvers
PROJECT— Bad I.D. of incoming customer tapes
SOLUTION— Standardized labels, letter sent to customers explaining new labeling system
BENEFITS— Fewer labels; reduction of time spent identifying tapes; $15,000 cost savings
NUMBER OF HOURS TO COMPLETE—19

---

[*] This number is the result of multiplying the number of members by the number of meetings.

TABLE 5.6

Measurable Cost Savings
Check Processing

Division	Cost Savings		Cost		Net
Demand Deposit Services	$ 20,000.00	−	$24,000.00	=	$−4,000.00
Document Processing Center	84,213.00	−	30,783.00	=	$ 53,430.00
Proof	8,626.00	−	4,944.00	=	3,682.00
Remittance Banking Division	14,450.00	−	11,122.00	=	3,328.00
Bank Card	28,000.00	−	9,917.00	=	18,083.00
Total:	$155,289.00		$80,766.00		$ 74,523.00

TABLE 5.7

Team Projects

	Quality	Productivity	Work Area	Service	$
Year one	17	15	7	15	$ 161,500
Year two	33	40	16	30	$1,194,400
Total:	50	55	23	45	$1,255,900
%:	(29%)	(32%)	(13%)	(26%)	

Accepted projects year one	54
Accepted projects year two	119
Total:	173

Project Acceptance Rate: 98% (173/177)

TABLE 5.8

Completed Projects by Area

Department	Number of Projects	Quality	Productivity	Work Area	Service	$
Bond/Trust	3	1	2	—	—	$ 34,000
Charge Card	36	10	7	10	9	$ 128,000
Item Processing	19	6	7	3	3	$ 755,300
Controllers	9	3	3	—	3	$ 101,100
Operations	95	28	31	10	26	$ 67,500
Customer Services	3	—	2	—	1	19,800
Personnel	4	1	—	—	3	100,000
Data Processing	4	1	3	—	—	50,200
Total:	173	50	55	23	45	$1,255,900

TABLE 5.9

Quality Bookkeeping System
Bookkeeping Services

Defect/Central Subject	This Period's Defect Ratio	This Period's Defect %	Standard	QCI Unweighted	Weight	QCI Weighted
Wrong Account Number/ Total Deposits	76/36,834	0.2	0.1	58		
Nonendorsed Deposits/ Total Deposits	113/37,836	0.3	0.3	106		
Input Quality						
Missing Items/Total Statements	60/49,538	0.12*	0.06	67	6	462
Stop Payment Incorrect/ Total Stop Payments	6/2,376	0.25	0.25	104	5	520
Misfiled Items/Total Checks and Debits	34/236,790	0.01	0.01	108	4 (15)	400 / 1,382
Internal Quality Performance						68%
Wrong Statement Sent/ Total Statements	14/49,538	0.83	0.82	67	4	268
Missing Items/Total Statements	4/49,538	0.006*	0.004	50	3	150
Incorrect Adjustments/ Total Statements	33/49,538	0.07	0.06	96	6 (12)	430 / 848
External Quality Performance						71%
Overall Quality Performance					(27)	2,170 / 80%

* out of control

good items produced over the amount of resources that are used to produce that item. An example of a basic measure would be the number of correct pages typed over the number of labor hours actually required to do all the typing necessary to get the correct pages. These labor hours would also include the number of hours spent retyping a page or correcting errors in order to complete the correct pages.

Most supervisors are primarily responsible for labor hours; however, in some cases, they may be responsible for other resources such as materials, supplies, or other production variables. If these are also under the responsibility of the supervisor, then these should also be productivity measures. A second productivity measure in this case could be the number of correct pages typed over the number of pieces of paper being used to complete the number of correct pages. Multiple resources can also be combined into a single measure. The following is the basic formula for a productivity measurement on tickets processed:

Productivity Measurement

$$\frac{\text{Tickets Processed}}{\text{Labor} + \text{Systems} + \text{Forms}} =$$

$$\frac{2080 \text{ tickets}}{(\$11.13 \text{ per hour} \times 640 \text{ hours}) + (\text{systems charges } \$500 \text{ per month}) +} =$$

$$\frac{2,080}{(\$11.13 \times 640) + \$500 + (\$.05 \times 2,600)} =$$

$$\frac{2,080}{\$7,123 + \$500 + \$130} = 26.83 \text{ (productivity index)}$$

Measurable Service Improvement

Service is also an important performance measure. An example of a *service measure* might be the average number of customers serviced per hour. In this case, the time to service all customers would be divided by the number of customers to determine the average time per customer. Another example of customer service might be the average amount of time needed to complete a customer inquiry or complaint by telephone or mail. In this case, it is important to keep track of the time and date each inquiry or complaint came in and when each was completed. The calendar days or hours to complete all inquiries or complaints are divided by the number of complaints to determine average response time.

A successful employee involvement process continuously improves the performance measures over time. For the quality measures the quality level should be expected to increase with a decrease in defects. If the department were at a 0.5 percent quality level the team would strive to lower the defect rate to about 0.4 percent. In terms of the productivity measures, the group could look toward increasing the productivity index by dividing the resource volume (labor hours or sheets of paper) into the number of correct pages produced hoping to increase the index. If the index was 0.9 percent (ninety correct pages/one hundred pieces of paper) then the productivity index should be increased to 0.91 percent or better. However, this increase should not be at the expense of quality.

To improve performance in customer service, the average time to service a customer and the average investigation time should decrease. These would all be positive tangible signs that the team members are not only completing successful projects directly affecting their work, but also improving their attitude and individual actions toward their work and the customer. Members are working more like a team helping each other, working toward the same goals and objectives, and applying the same problem-solving techniques they learned as a group.

These measures also reflect a secondary or increased return on the projects teams are accomplishing. In many cases, it may be difficult to truly determine the new quality level, new productivity level, and the new customer service level that a particular project may yield, but these measures will bring together both the results of those projects that have been implemented and the other skills and abilities of the team members. By setting up and monitoring these performance measures prior to and after establishing teams in an environment with minimal changes, they can be additional direct measures of team results.

Tables 5.10 and 5.11 show both tangible and intangible benefits as performance improvement.

Improvement in Work Environment

Another set of measures that falls into the tangible, but indirect category is absenteeism, turnover, safety, and grievances. These are classified as such because even if the work environment is highly stable, there may be other factors in the external environment that affect the individuals and cause changes in these measures.

TABLE 5.10

Tangible Achievements

Quality	*Performance to Standard* (%)	*Service Defect Rate* (%)
Chk. Proc.	↑ 22%	↓ 11.3%
GBS Ops.	↑ 1.45%	↓ 96%
Bankwide	↑ 13%	↓ 17%

Customer Service

	Turnaround Time (days)
Chk. Proc.	↓ 10.03%
GBS Ops.	↓ 30.3%
Bankwide	↓ 12.5%

Some examples might be financial or family situations, the economy, and individual priorities, goals and objectives.

Absenteeism can be measured by dividing the number of nonholiday and nonvacation days absent by the number of total days scheduled for work during the period. Turnover is measured by dividing the number of employees that have left a particular area by the total number employed in the area for a given period. For both of these measures, decreasing percentages are a sign of improvement. Safety is measured by the number of accidents that have occurred for the period. Grievances are measured in the same way. An alternate way to measure these would be to divide the number of accidents or grievances by the number of people employed for the period. This method only makes sense if the number of people employed from period to period changes significantly. These measures will be affected positively as the participative process gets people more involved, satisfied with their jobs, and motivated toward organizational and individual development goals. While unions are more evident in manufacturing organizations, they may also be present in a service industry. The benefits of employee involvement from a union perspective may include fewer grievances, more open communication, less absenteeism, better working conditions, and improved product quality without manpower loss.

Individual Measurement

Up to this point, the measures discussed have monitored the results of the program for the organization itself. It is also essential for the long-term success of any employee involvement team and for the good of the organization that individuals receive a positive, measurable benefit from the process. One way to determine whether individuals are receiving a net benefit would be for managers to observe members and make subjective judgments or discuss team involvement with employees. However, these approaches do not bring together the overall benefits that are being accrued to the individuals and the team.

A better way to approach the measure of individual accrued benefits would be to develop a survey-type measurement instrument for team members and nonmembers in which they could record their attitudes and feelings. Then it could be statistically determined what changes, if any, have taken place from the perspective of team members and other employees. The best way to approach this would be to develop a survey that is longitudinal in nature. This survey could be administered prior to the establishment of participative teams to establish a base for each individual and the group and then repeated six months or one year after the establishment of teams. This may also be repeated one or two years after the second administration of the survey.

The survey instrument provides a benchmark against which each individual and the team as a whole can be measured in terms of changes in attitude. The net benefits being gained by individuals as they continue to learn and apply their skills in the teams should also be evident. Not only is it useful to survey the individuals about their feelings and perceptions, and how they have changed, but it is also helpful to survey managers about the benefits of the teams, as well as the benefits to the organization.

Two surveys that have been used in major organizations are included (Figures 5.2 and 5.3) at the end of this chapter. These questions can be used as they are, or they can be modified and administered as the situation and organization dictate. The survey given to the team members (Figure 5.2) can be used as a longitudinal measure given before the group begins and repeated periodically. This survey can be administered directly to members and nonmembers with their knowledge that this is an assessment to determine the before-and-after effects of participative teams. Another approach is to administer the survey to all work group members, those people who are not team members and those who are. In this case, employees do not know that this is a survey measuring the before-and-after effects. This approach will eliminate any bias and determine if there is a true correlation between teams and the individual factors.

This survey has been effective in measuring employee attitudes on the benefits they derive in teams from period to period. The results of both surveys have shown that team members are often more positive on all factors than nonmembers. Nonmembers in areas that have teams are more positive than nonmembers that do not have teams in their area (test group). When given covertly, a significant correlation is also established between team membership and positive perception and improvement of factors such as job satisfaction, morale, communications, interpersonal relationships, reference groups, responsibility, challenge, personal growth, trust, reward and recognition, and teamwork.

The results of this survey parallel an American Management Association research study on participation groups that also reported significant results in terms of attitudes and behavior. The study showed the following benefits:

- Increased individual self-respect
- Increased the respect for employees by supervisor
- Increased employee understanding of the difficulties faced by supervisors
- Changed some employees' negative attitudes
- Reduced conflict stemming from the work environment
- Increased employee understanding of why many problems are not solved quickly

The management survey is of equal importance. The survey is administered to those managers, supervisors and above (the entire management team), who are involved in the participative process as well as a number of managers and supervisors who are not involved in the process so that a test group is established. The managers are asked to respond to a number of questions about their experience with the team process, if they are involved in the process, and their perceptions if they are not involved in the process. A sample survey is included (Figure 5.3).

Management's responses typically are more positive at higher levels of the organization than at lower levels. Even at lower levels there is often a positive feeling about the effects of the participative process on the people, the work unit, and the organization. This management survey can also be given longitudinally to see what changes are taking place in management's perception of the process from period to period. If there is a downward trend in the survey, or on particular question response, then it is important to investigate that trend to find out why managements' perceptions have changed. If the program is administered and supported effectively, managerial perceptions of the process should begin and continue to be positive, particularly if the measures discussed earlier are communicated effectively throughout the organization.

Questions for the management survey focus on communications, quality, morale, service, productivity, costs, teamwork, standards, problem solving, projects, leadership skills, training, and reward and recognition. These questions can be computer analyzed with frequencies, percentages, and cross tabulation of results. Tests of significance may also be made. Computer statistical packages such as SPSS and SAS are helpful in analyzing survey data.

Computers in Measurement

Computers can be extremely useful in most phases of the measurement process. The process measures that were discussed including the recording of trainees, members, participative teams, manpower levels, project selections, completed projects with their benefits and costs, and reward and recognition can all be recorded on word processing equipment and can be continuously and easily updated with new information.

A personal computer or a microcomputer is used almost the same way as a word processor to hold the information and to update materials. In addition, calculations are executed and hard-copy printed as necessary for distribution. If electronic mail or multiple terminals are available, raw data on projects, members, and teams can be sent via computer to the person who is compiling the measurement information. An electronic form can input directly to a calculation matrix. The report information is calculated automatically, updated, and available for hard-copy reports or visual display on the terminal screen.

A microcomputer with or without electronic mail and/or electronic forms can be used effectively and efficiently to track quality, productivity, and service level measures. Absenteeism and turnover rates, as well as safety and grievance occurrences, can be measured with immediate updating and retrieval. In addition, graphing packages or modules are available to effectively display the data. All of these applications have been used to measure and report the results of employee involvement teams.

Reporting Results of Measurement

The results of measurement should be made available to the teams. The power of reporting positive results to these groups should not be underestimated. It can be extremely motivational for team members to see the results of their efforts— not only the direct results of the projects that the team is working on, but the application in terms of quality and productivity, customer service, absenteeism, turnover, safety, and grievances. Seeing how they are contributing to the organization can give team members additional job satisfaction. These measures also may lead the teams to new projects and issues.

It is important to caution that the collection of numbers for the measures should not be the end in itself. These are simply indicators of the effectiveness of the teams and the participative process, and not the only reason for the teams or the process. It is the means that justifies the end; not the end that justifies the means. Therefore, it is essential to communicate all of these measures to the teams in a clear and understandable manner. The measures can be a self-fulfilling prophecy; if management and team members want the measures to look good, they will. The teams more than anyone else want measurement to show results.

It is also critical to communicate the results of the measures to management at all levels. The lifeblood of the participative process is measurement. Management will continue to support the employee involvement process as it sees positive results through the measures. Results also should be communicated to all parts of the company, not just those areas using the participative process. This provides information to those in the organization not using participative teams so they have a positive view of the process and are more supportive and helpful when the teams are soliciting their support and assistance. This may help bring other areas of the company into the participative process. Company newspapers, bulletins, or publications specifically devoted to reporting on employee involvement can also be useful in sharing results.

Communicating the results of the participative process outside the company can also be valuable. This information is persuasive to customers and potential customers when they know that improvements are taking place that will affect the products and services they use. Additionally, customers and potential customers will also be impressed with the attitude of the company, the progressiveness, and desire to improve employees as well as products. Employee development and the corporate attitude this represents will also be viewed positively by potential job candidates. They will seek employment with a company that allows employees to maximize their skills and abilities and to participate in the planning and decision making of the company.

Measurement simply cannot be overlooked or underestimated. It is extremely important to all aspects of a healthy participative process. Organizations that have been most successful with employee involvement have made a substantial investment in the measurement process and have effectively communicated and utilized the results of measurement.

FIGURE 5.2

Employee Survey

The purpose of this questionnaire is to assess the attitudes our employees have toward work, relationships with management and co-workers, organizational environment, and personal development.

Please answer each question as accurately and honestly as possible. Do not spend too much time with any one question. Your initial reactions are probably your most accurate.

The questions are designed to obtain *your* perceptions of your job and *your* reactions to it. This is not a test; it is an opportunity to assess your job satisfaction. All information gathered from this survey will be recorded anonymously and will be strictly confidential.

We appreciate your assistance in furthering our understanding of employee attitudes by completing this survey.

I. *Instructions:* Please put an "x" in the appropriate box.

Sex
    1. Male   ☐
    2. Female   ☐

Age
    1. Under 20 years old   ☐
    2. 20–24 years old   ☐
    3. 25–34 years old   ☐
    4. 35–49 years old   ☐
    5. 50–64 years old   ☐
    6. 65 years old or older   ☐

Classification
    1. Full-time   ☐
    2. Part-time   ☐

Years of Service
    1. Less than 6 mos.   ☐
    2. 6 mos. to 1 year   ☐
    3. 1–2 years   ☐
    4. 2–4 years   ☐
    5. 4–8 years   ☐
    6. Over 8 years   ☐

Years in Current Section
    1. Less than 6 mos.   ☐
    2. 6 mos. to 1 year   ☐
    3. 1–2 years   ☐
    4. 2–4 years   ☐
    5. 4–8 years   ☐
    6. Over 8 years   ☐

Years in Salary Grade
    1. Less than 6 mos.   ☐
    2. 6 mos. to 1 year   ☐
    3. 1–2 years   ☐
    4. 2–4 years   ☐
    5. 4–8 years   ☐
    6. Over 8 years   ☐

1	2	3	4	5	6	7	8	9	10	11

Salary Grade (check one)

FIGURE 5.2 (Continued)

Race or Nationality

1. White ☐
2. Black ☐
3. Hispanic ☐
4. Oriental ☐
5. Other: _____

Additional Activities (check Yes *or* No regarding your active participation during the past year)

	Yes	No
1. Do you participate in the Suggestion Award System?	☐	☐
2. Are you a member of the Ski Club?	☐	☐
3. Are you a member in the 25 Year Club?	☐	☐
4. Are you a Quality Team Member?	☐	☐
5. Do you participate in our club activities (e.g., flower show, golf outing, etc.)?	☐	☐
6. Do you participate in the PALS Program?	☐	☐
7. Do you participate in the Food Drive?	☐	☐
8. Do you participate in the Clothing Drive?	☐	☐
9. Are you a member of a softball team?	☐	☐
10. Do you belong to the bowling league?	☐	☐

II. Following are a set of statements related to your *overall* opinion of our organization. Please read each statement carefully. Circle the *one* number that most closely reflects how you feel about that statement.

	Strongly Disagree	Generally Disagree	Generally Agree	Strongly Agree
1. Our organization has a reputation for high standards.	1	2	3	4
2. Employee policies and procedures are followed only when essential.	1	2	3	4
3. The rewards and encouragement we get are normally more frequent than the criticism and/or threats.	1	2	3	4
4. There is something about working for this organization that encourages me to do my best.	1	2	3	4
5. Employees of this organization are generally pleasant and friendly.	1	2	3	4
6. Our quality and productivity suffer because of poor planning and organization.	1	2	3	4
7. Most employees take pride in being a member of this organization.	1	2	3	4
8. This organization subscribes to the philosophy of striving for constant improvement.	1	2	3	4
9. Most employees in our organization trust each other.	1	2	3	4
10. Management is flexible enough that innovations are encouraged and will receive consideration.	1	2	3	4

FIGURE 5.2 (Continued)

III. These statements will assess how important certain attributes of the organization are to *you*. Please read each statement carefully. Circle the *one* number that most accurately describes your feeling about that statement.

	Strongly Disagree	Generally Disagree	Generally Agree	Strongly Agree
1. Good relations with my co-workers are very important to me.	1	2	3	4
2. Recognition from management for a job well done is very important to me.	1	2	3	4
3. A high salary is not the most important part of my employment.	1	2	3	4
4. I do not like to make decisions affecting my job.	1	2	3	4
5. Doing interesting work is very important to me.	1	2	3	4

IV. The following statements are related to your satisfaction with different aspects of *your* job. Please read each statement carefully. Circle the *one* number that best describes your feeling about that statement.

	Strongly Disagree	Generally Disagree	Generally Agree	Strongly Agree
1. I enjoy doing my work.	1	2	3	4
2. I am not happy with the pay and benefits I receive.	1	2	3	4
3. In doing my job, I get a lot of opportunity for personal growth and development.	1	2	3	4
4. I like the people I work with on my job.	1	2	3	4
5. I receive a great degree of respect and fair treatment from my boss.	1	2	3	4
6. I get a feeling of worthwhile accomplishment from my job.	1	2	3	4
7. I do not have a lot of friends at work.	1	2	3	4
8. I never need to think creatively on my job.	1	2	3	4
9. My physical surroundings are pleasant to work in.	1	2	3	4
10. I receive a great amount of support and guidance from my supervisor.	1	2	3	4
11. My chances for promotion are nonexistent.	1	2	3	4
12. I always receive enough time, information, and materials to complete my work.	1	2	3	4
13. I work with my co-workers as a team.	1	2	3	4
14. I do not participate in many decisions that affect my work.	1	2	3	4
15. The factor that contributes the most to my personal job satisfaction is:				

Thank you for completing this survey.

FIGURE 5.3

Management Survey

The purpose of this survey is to determine attitudes toward quality teams results, participation, and training. The results of this survey will be used to assist the Quality Assurance Division in making improvements in the quality team process.

Please answer each question as accurately and honestly as possible. The questionnaire takes approximately twenty minutes to complete. Do not spend too much time with any one question. Your initial reactions are probably the most accurate.

All information gathered from this questionnaire will be recorded anonymously and will be strictly confidential. Thank you for your assistance in furthering our understanding of attitudes toward quality teams.

SECTION I

Please check the appropriate box(es).

LEVEL IN ORGANIZATION

1. OGM ☐
2. AOGM ☐
3. DIV MGR ☐
4. ASST MGR ☐
5. MGR SUPR ☐
6. SUPR ☐
7. STAFF ☐

SERVICE

1. Less than 1 year ☐
2. 1–2 years ☐
3. 3–4 years ☐
4. 5–10 years ☐
5. 11–15 years ☐
6. Over 15 years ☐

TIME INVOLVED WITH QUALITY TEAMS

1. No involvement ☐
2. 1–2 months ☐
3. 2–4 months ☐
4. 5–6 months ☐
5. 7 months–1 year ☐
6. Over 1 year ☐

RELATIONSHIP TO TEAMS
(check all that apply)

1. Manager ☐
2. Steering Committee ☐
3. Facilitator ☐
4. Leader ☐
5. Member ☐
6. No Relationship ☐

SECTION II

The following statements are related to quality team results. Please read each statement carefully. Circle the *one* number that best describes your feelings about the statement.

	Strongly Disagree	Generally Disagree	No Opinion	Generally Agree	Strongly Agree
1. Quality teams help promote better communication between managers and employees.	1	2	3	4	5
2. Quality team projects can reduce errors in the work area.	1	2	3	4	5
3. Quality teams help to increase employee morale.	1	2	3	4	5
4. Quality team projects contribute toward providing better service to our customers.	1	2	3	4	5
5. Quality team projects help increase work productivity.	1	2	3	4	5
6. Quality teams help promote better communication among employees.	1	2	3	4	5
7. Quality teams waste employees' time.	1	2	3	4	5

FIGURE 5.3 (Continued)

	Strongly Disagree	Generally Disagree	No Opinion	Generally Agree	Strongly Agree
8. Quality team projects can help reduce costs for our organization.	1	2	3	4	5
9. Quality teams help promote effective employee teamwork.	1	2	3	4	5
10. Quality team projects help to increase employee awareness of quality standards.	1	2	3	4	5
11. The quality of work improved in our work area after implementation of quality team recommendations.	1	2	3	4	5

SECTION III

The following statements are related to participation in the Quality team process. Please read each statement carefully. Circle the *one* number that best describes your feelings about the statement.

	Strongly Disagree	Generally Disagree	No Opinion	Generally Agree	Strongly Agree
1. Quality teams take too much time away from work activities.	1	2	3	4	5
2. I participate in quality team project presentations.	1	2	3	4	5
3. I frequently attend quality team meetings.	1	2	3	4	5
4. I feel forced to support quality teams.	1	2	3	4	5
5. Employees regard quality teams as a way to get out of work.	1	2	3	4	5
6. Employees view quality teams as a way for the organization to get extra work from them.	1	2	3	4	5
7. Employees feel forced to participate in quality teams.	1	2	3	4	5
8. Employees show enthusiasm toward quality teams.	1	2	3	4	5
9. Employees will fall behind in their work if they participate in quality teams.	1	2	3	4	5
10. I enthusiastically support quality team activities.	1	2	3	4	5
11. Quality teams lessen my authority over my employees.	1	2	3	4	5
12. Participation in quality teams should be mandatory.	1	2	3	4	5

SECTION IV

These final statements are related to Quality team training. Please read each statement carefully. Circle the *one* number that best describes your feeling about the statement.

	Strongly Disagree	Generally Disagree	No Opinion	Generally Agree	Strongly Agree
1. Quality teams help employees develop effective problem-solving capabilities.	1	2	3	4	5

FIGURE 5.3 (Continued)

	Strongly Disagree	Generally Disagree	No Opinion	Generally Agree	Strongly Agree
2. Quality teams select projects that are beneficial to the work area.	1	2	3	4	5
3. Quality teams help employees develop leadership skills.	1	2	3	4	5
4. Employees receive adequate training in quality team problem-solving techniques.	1	2	3	4	5
5. Employees are a good resource for solving problems in the work area.	1	2	3	4	5
6. Managers receive sufficient information concerning feedback and awards used to respond to and recognize quality team recommendations.	1	2	3	4	5
7. Managers receive adequate training in quality team problem-solving techniques.	1	2	3	4	5
8. Additional training in problem-solving techniques is needed for managers after six months of involvement with quality teams.	1	2	3	4	5
9. Employees receive sufficient training to prepare project presentations for management.	1	2	3	4	5
10. Additional training in problem-solving techniques is needed for employees after six months of involvement with quality teams.	1	2	3	4	5
11. Quality teams in this organization will continue to be an ongoing process.	1	2	3	4	5

Thank you for completing this survey.

TABLE 5.11

Intangible Benefits

- Improve communication
- Increase problem-solving skills
- Enhance teamwork
- Develop leadership capabilities
- Better management/employee relationships
- Promote personal growth/development
- Improve attitude and morale
- Increase job knowledge/awareness
- Improve job satisfaction
- Increase employee motivation and commitment

Additional Reading

American Insurance Company. *Quality Improvement Techniques.* New York: American Management Association, 1962.

American Society for Quality Control. *Quality Costs—What & How.* 2d ed. Milwaukee, WI:ASQC, 1971.

Amsden, D. N., and R. T. Amsden, eds. *QC Circles: Applications, Tools and Theory.* Milwaukee, WI: American Society for Quality Control, 1976.

Anderson, V. N. "Five Steps to Quality Control of Clerical Operations." *Systems and Procedures Journal,* Nov. and Dec. 1964: 8–12.

Aubrey, Charles A. II. "Using Quality Circles in Banking." *Enterprising Ideas,* 1(2):11–12.

_____. *Quality Management in Financial Services.* Wheaton, IL.: Hitchcock Executive Book Service, Hitchcock Publishing Co., 1985.

_____. "Stressing Quality—The Path to Productivity." *The Magazine of Bank Administration,* June 1983: 20–24.

_____. "Quality Circles in Banking." *The Southern Banker,* May 1982: 30–32.

Aubrey, Charles A. II, and Lawrence A. Eldridge. "Stressing Quality—The Path to Productivity." *Systems and Procedures Journal,* Nov. and Dec. 1964: 8–12.

_____. "Banking on High Quality." *Quality Progress,* Dec. 1981: 14–19.

Aubrey, Charles A. II, and Wendy C. Fencl. "Management Professional and Clerical Quality Circles." *36th Annual Quality Congress Transactions,* May 1982.

Aubrey, Charles A. II, and Laurie A. Hirsch. "Implementation, Operation, and Results of Bank Circles." *3rd Annual International Association of Quality Circles Conference Transactions,* April, 1983.

Aubrey, Charles A. II, and Debra A. Zimbler. "The Banking Industry: Quality Costs and Improvements." *Quality Progress,* Dec. 1983: 16–20.

_____. "Quality + or − Quality Costs Equals Productivity." *37th Annual Quality Congress Transactions,* May, 1983.

_____. "A Banking Quality Cost Model, Its Uses and Results." *36th Annual Quality Congress Transactions,* May 1982.

Barkman, Donald F. "Team Discipline: Put Performance on the Line." *Personnel Journal,* 66(3):58–63. March 1987.

Barra, Ralph. *Putting Quality Circles to Work.* New York: McGraw-Hill Book Company, 1983.

"Basic Tools for Clerical Quality Control." *Twenty-seventh Annual Conference Proceedings.* New Brunswick, NJ: Metropolitan Section, American Society for Quality Control, 1968.

Beardsley, J. F., and D. L. Dewar. *Quality Circles.* Cupertino, CA.: International Association of Quality Circles, 1978.

Benz, William M. "Quality Control in the Office." *Industrial Quality Control* 23(11):531–34.

Berger, Roger W. "Developing Quality Information Systems." *Administration Application Division of the American Society for Quality Control 1976 Yearbook.* Hot Springs, AR: S. G. Johnson, 1976.

Bergstrom, James. *Teller Differences Rate, A Study of Factors Affecting Teller Performance.* Park Ridge, IL: Bank Administration Institute, 1976.

Brown, A. W. "Professionalism—Let's Give It a New Dimension." *Administrative Application Division of the American Society for Quality Control 1975 Yearbook.* Milwaukee, WI:ASQC, 1975.

Carter, Jr., C. L. "Results and How to Get Them." *Administrative Application Division of the American Society for Quality Control 1976 Yearbook.* Hot Springs, AR: S. G. Johnson, 1976.

"Clerical Process Capability." *Twenty-fifth Annual Conference Proceedings.* New Brunswick, NJ: Metropolitan Section, American Society for Quality Control, 1972.

Cole, R. E. *Diffusion of New Work Structures in Japan.* University of Michigan, presented before the First Annual International Conference on Quality Circles. San Francisco, Feb. 15–16, 1979.

———. *Work Mobility and Participation: A Comparative Study of American and Japanese Industry.* University of California Press, 1979.

Crosby, Philip B. *Cutting the Cost of Quality.* Boston: Industrial Education Institute, 1967.

———. *Quality is Free: The Art of Making Quality Certain.* New York: McGraw-Hill Book Co., 1979.

Dawes, Edgar W. "Optimizing Attribute Sampling Cost." *Twenty-seventh Annual Technical Conference Transactions of the American Society for Quality Control,* 1973.

Day, Carl A. "What Can Management Expect from Quality Control." *Quality Control in Action,* Report no. 9. American Management Association, 1958: 17.

Deming, William Edwards. *Some Theory of Sampling.* New York: John Wiley & Sons, 1950.

———. "Some Statistical Logic in the Management of Quality." *All India Conference on Quality Control Proceedings,* New Delhi, May 1971.

Dertinger, E. F. "Quality Assurance: A New Organizational Concept." *New Concepts in Manufacturing Management.* New York: American Management Association, 1961.

Dumas, Roland A., Nancy Cushing and Carol Laughlin "Making Quality Control Theories Workable." *Training & Development Journal.* 41(2): 30–33. Feb. 1987.

Employee Involvement in Quality and Productivity, Chicago. B. J. Chakiris Corporation, 1985.

Evans, Gordon H. "Manufacturing Staff Services." *Supervisory Management, Managerial Job Descriptions in Manufacturing.* New York: American Management Association, 1964.

Exton, Jr., William. "How to Improve Clerical Accuracy." *Supervisory Management,* April 1971: 30.

Feigenbaum, A. V. *Total Quality Control Engineering and Management.* New York: McGraw-Hill Book Co., 1961.

Fetter, Robert B. *The Quality Control System.* Homewood, IL: Richard D. Irwin, Inc., 1967.

Fukuda, Ryuji. *Managerial Engineering: Techniques for Improving Quality and Productivity in the Workplace.* Stamford, CN: Productivity, Inc., 1983.

Groocock, J. M. *The Cost of Quality.* New York: Pitman Publishing, Inc., 1974.

Gryna, Jr., Frank M. *Quality Circles: A Team Approach to Problem Solving.* New York: AMACOM, 1981.

Hagan, John T. *A Management Role for Quality Control.* New York: American Management Association, 1968.

Hubbard, James. "Primary Research Interviewing Techniques." *Bank Marketing,* July 1978: 40–53.

Ingle, Sud and Ingle, Nima. *Quality Circles in Service Industries.* Englewood Cliffs, NJ: Prentice-Hall, Inc., 1983.

Ishikawa, Kaoru. *Guide to Quality Control.* Tokyo: Asian Productivity Organization, 1976.

Juran, J. M. *Quality Control Handbook.* 3d ed. New York: McGraw-Hill Book Co., 1974.

Juran, J. M., and F. M. Gryna. *Quality Planning and Analysis from Product Development through Use.* New York: McGraw-Hill Book Co., 1980.

Kelly, Patrick J. "Using the Semantic Differential." *Bank Marketing,* Sept. 1973: 25–28.

Kirby E. "Quality Control in Banking." *Administrative Application Division of the American Society for Quality Control 1975 Yearbook.* Hot Springs, AR: S. G. Johnson, 1976.

Langevin, Roger G. *Quality Control in the Service Industries.* Management Briefing. New York: American Management Association, 1977.

Latzko, William J. "A Quality Control System for Banks." *The Magazine of Bank Administration,* Nov. 1972: 17–23.

_____. "Quality Control in Banking." *Twenty-fourth Annual Conference Proceedings.* New Brunswick, NJ: Metropolitan Section, American Society for Quality Control, 1972.

MacBryde, Vernon. "Controlling the Cost of Quality." *Administrative Application Division of the American Society for Quality Control 1976 Yearbook.* Hot Springs, AR: S. G. Johnson, 1976.

Mears, Peter. "An Empirical Investigation of Banking Customers' Perception of Bank Machines." *Journal of Bank Research,* Summer 1978: 112–15.

Mills, Ted. "Europe's Industrial Democracy: An American Response." *Harvard Business Review,* Nov.–Dec. 1978: 143–52.

Murdock, Bennett B. "Quality Control in Clerical Operations." *Leadership in the Office.* New York: American Management Association, 1963.

Niland, Powell. *The Quality Control Circle: An Analysis.* Singapore: McGraw-Hill Far Eastern Publishers (s) Ltd., 1971.

Olmstead, Blair E. "Quality Control Applied to Clerical Operations." *Twenty-second Annual Conference.* New Brunswick, NJ: American Society for Quality Control, 1970.

Ott, Ellis R. *Process Quality Control.* New York: McGraw-Hill Book Co., 1975.

Parnell, E. M. "Self-Examination—The Achilles' Heel of Teams." *Supervision.* 49(2): 6–8. Feb. 1987.

Publisher of Japan. *Quality Control Circle Case Studies.* Japan: Asian Productivity Organization, 1972.

"Quality Control of Service—The 1974 Japanese Symposium." *Quality Progress* 8(4): 10–13.

"QUIP—The Quality Improvement Program." *Twenty-ninth Annual Technical Conference Proceedings.* Boston: American Society for Quality Control, 1975.

"Reducing Clerical Quality Costs." *Twenty-eighth Annual Technical Conference Proceedings.* Boston: American Society for Quality Control, 1974.

Ruffner, Esher R. and Lawrence P. Ettkin. "When a Circle Is Not a Circle." *Advanced Management Journal,* 52(2): 9–15. Spring, 1987.

Sheldon, George, and Frederick E. Finch. "Bank Queues: A Comparative Analysis of Waiting Lines." *Magazine of Bank Administration,* July 1976: 31–35.

Shewhart, W. A. *Economic Control of Quality of Manufactured Product.* Princeton, NJ: van Nostrand Company, 1931.

Simmons, David A. *Practical Quality Control.* Reading, MA: Addison-Wesley Publishing Co., 1970.

Smith, Martin R. *Qualitysense: Organizational Approaches to Improving Product Quality and Service.* New York: American Management Association, 1979.

Staab, Thomas C. "Quality Applicable to Paperwork?—Probably!" *Twenty-seventh Annual Technical Transaction.* Milwaukee, WI: American Society for Quality Control, 1973.

Thompson, Philip C. *Quality Circles: How to Make Them Work in America.* New York: AMACOM, 1982.

Townsend, Patrick L. with Joan E. Gebhardt. *Commit to Quality.* New York: John Wiley & Sons, Inc., 1986.

Trapp, Brian E. "The Building of an Effective MICR Quality Control Program." *Twenty-ninth Annual Technical Conference Proceedings.* San Diego, CA: American Society for Quality Control, 1975.

Van Horne, James C. *Financial Management and Policy.* 2d ed. Englewood Cliffs, NJ: Prentice Hall, 1971.

CHAPTER 6
Special Uses of Participative Teams

The most predictable aspect of modern organizations is that they must deal with change. Economic, social, and technological changes are affecting and will continue to affect work and management within the organization. American workers have traditionally looked to the organization and their work to give them identity, direction, development, and success. Future workers are likely to be more active, sophisticated, and demanding employees.

Jobs matching the skills of current employees and the total number of jobs will probably decrease in future years. Jobs that are available one year may not have existed the year before. Employees as well as organizations will have to make adjustments to meet these challenges. Success in work may also have to be defined in a different way. There may be less connection to the work ethic and traditional career concepts, and more commitment to self-development. However, there will be opportunities for individual development and satisfaction within the organization as well as in the community. Because of this, the relationship between work and leisure will be more significant. The drive for financial success may also decrease in importance as people seek more individual growth, development, and satisfaction from their work inside and outside the organization.

A review of popular *megatrends* suggests major shifts in attitudes and actions that apply to many aspects of our lives including both individual and organizational development.[22] There are obvious implications for greater employee involvement within the organization. In the past, most of the participative process has been concentrated in the manufacturing industry with quality circles and similar problem-solving groups. Today, with the shift from an industrial society to a post-industrial society, the majority of all jobs are service based. Opportunities for future innovation in quality and productivity improvement in the service industry are substantial.

Advances in technology power the growth in information services. While technology may increase efficiency and capacity, technology also makes many jobs less personal. Information specialists may spend all day working at a computer terminal. In spite of all efforts at developing a user-friendly system, many employees still feel some apprehension in using computers. Yet success may be based on some ability to interact with a sophisticated computer system. The increasing stress of keeping pace with change and the impersonal elements of technological complexity create a corresponding need in employees for some personal recognition, support, and opportunity for influence. Filling some of those needs is one way management can maintain employee commitment and motivation for quality and productivity improvement.

Future Trends

The organization of the future must be flexible and strong because it will be in a constant state of change. Wasteful, inefficient, and rigid organizations will cease to exist, and more productive and innovative organizations will take their place. In this process, there will be basic changes in work and organizational structure. Traditional roles and relationships between employees and supervisors may be modified in a decentralized organization with fewer formal power hierarchies. The ideal manager will be a facilitator, counselor, and coordinator in the task of developing employee competence.

The following list is a compilation of the views of many experts who present their vision of the future of work and the work environment.[1–7,9–11,13–17,19–21,25] Many of these changes are already evident. Most support a continuing emphasis on the participative process with increased employee involvement in problem solving and decision making. Future trends in work may include the following:

- Organizational power pushed to lower levels
- Decentralized organizational structure and decision making
- Increased emphasis on service industries
- Line supervisors who take more responsibility as a teacher and resource for their employees
- Employee profit sharing
- Employee ownership and membership on board of directors
- Increased power to consumers and constituents
- International management teams
- Autonomous work teams and entrepreneurial groups
- Increased emphasis on individual competence
- More fluid organizational structure
- Informal approach to work
- Flexible working hours
- More attractive, humanized work areas
- More time spent in leisure-work
- A wider degree of diversity among employees
- Increased number of people working outside the organization

- Organizational concern for the health and fitness of employees

- Recognition of individual need for self-fulfillment and growth

- Greater rewards for innovation and creativity within the organization

These trends point to several options and opportunities for employee involvement in problem-solving and information-gathering teams. Thus the group itself becomes a primary vehicle for employee development inside the organization and in the community outside the organization. However, the teams must also evolve and develop by considering broader issues and taking more responsibility for decision making. This brings the organization closer to true participative management.

All groups go through progressive changes and periods of conflict. If quality teams or involvement groups have limited influence and scope, they will eventually reach a point where they must go through a process of renewal and evolve into a different kind of group, or the team may cease to exist. Several articles have been written about the life cycle of quality teams. P. R. Richardson compares the process to traditional courtship patterns and lists the following stages: (1) arousal of management interest, (2) courting of supervisory personnel, (3) courting of the work force, (4) consummation of union involvement, (5) romantic interlude during which employees express increased job interest, (6) complacency, and (7) program renewal or failure.[24]

E. E. Lawler and S. A. Mohrman suggest the following phases: start-up, initial problem solving, approval of initial suggestions, implementation, expansion of problem solving, and decline. However, they discuss the process of moving circles to other forms of participation including advisory groups, task forces, multi-level councils, business teams, and semiautonomous work groups. Figure 6.1, from Lawler and Mohrman, shows some of the directions for the evolution of participative groups.[12]

As participative groups evolve they seek wider responsibility in areas of policy, control, evaluation, and action. Some of the most significant opportunities for employee and management involvement are with the following groups:

- Task Force and Project Teams

- Autonomous and Self-Managing Work Teams

- Distributed Teams

- Issue Analysis Teams, Consumer Groups and Community Action Teams

Each of these types of participative teams will be discussed briefly in the following sections.

Task Force and Project Teams

These participative groups exist within many organizations today. These teams are comprised of experts and representatives from various parts of the organization.

FIGURE 6.1

Moving Circles to Other Forms of Participation

Type of Group

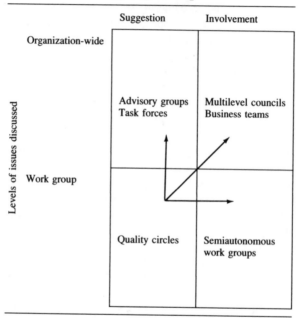

They come together for a limited period of time until a specific problem is solved or a special project is completed. The team may be asked to make suggestions or recommendations. Task coordination and cooperation among diverse individuals is essential in these groups.

These teams have many advantages in that they integrate the skills and knowledge of people from many areas of the organization. In some cases this link and interaction would not normally be made. These groups also facilitate communication and information exchange among different departments and areas of the organization. The combined efforts of these teams are usually better than any alone could produce.

Organizations are placing an increased emphasis on teamwork and cooperation in reaching organizational goals. In the future, organizations that are the most successful will have many rotating interactive teams. The teams will come together and then disengage as projects are completed and members go on to other teams. Many of these teams will involve management as well as other employees. Community members may also be a part of some groups. These teams are mainly operational with a basic task orientation. Their primary purpose is effective utilization and integration of organizational resources to meet task objectives, solve problems, and identify opportunities within the organization and the community.

Autonomous and Self-Managing Work Teams

Both short- and long-term autonomous teams working as independent, self-managed units with greater responsibility and specialized resources will become increasingly significant within the organization. These teams provide greater opportunities for individual self-development and create entrepreneurial spirit and innovation within a decentralized informal organization. In this situation, employees are responsible for a total process relating to a specific product or service. They work as a team, setting their own objectives, taking accountability for monitoring and evaluating their work, and making day-to-day decisions concerning that work. The team may deal with other departments as well as suppliers and customers.

Members of these teams should receive special training for this participation, including group dynamics and problem-solving techniques as well as advanced technical training. Members of the team also learn about different operations of the organization as they coordinate with other internal and external groups.

The implementation of self-managed teams is a complex process that may involve the redesign of a work system. As the organization becomes more differentiated, the greatest challenge is to integrate the separate parts to form natural coordinated units. One danger in developing autonomous groups is the potential for conflict and error if the segmented units have no interaction and functional links with other interrelated and interdependent groups. Effective communication, cooperation, and commitment are critical to the success of this self-managing process.

Distributed Teams

With growing trends toward decentralization and networking, employees may be in scattered sites and yet work as a team in problem solving and information sharing through computer conferencing. This distributed group may include those who work from computer terminals in their homes, but the primary emphasis is on full-time employees and resource personnel who are geographically dispersed throughout a formal organizational system.

These teams have interaction through a variety of computer communication formats including conferences, specialized forums, electronic mail, and bulletin boards. Groups can also meet through teleconferencing with audio and visual hookups to share ideas and analyze specific issues. The teleconference can be an impressive showcase for team efforts and presentations providing broad exposure and recognition to employees and management. However, because of the expense and effort involved in preparing for and implementing a video teleconference in several cities, this may be used less frequently than computer videotex conferencing or telephone conferencing.

The most economical method is often videotex computer teleconferencing. Team members work from their own microcomputers. They ask questions, answer questions, and provide information and responses by typing on their keyboards. Members of the team communicate almost instantaneously with any number of people. The team does need to observe some basic etiquette. They appoint a moderator, someone who knows the system, to ensure that everyone gets an opportunity to share information. If a member has a question, this can be indicated by typing a particular signal to the moderator.

Each team member can see the message on the screen as soon as it is sent. A printer also records a running transcript that can later be reviewed and edited. A number of other options are also available including group brainstorming and breaking out of a larger group into smaller subgroups.

The videotex system is effective in maintaining task orientation. There is no time or space for unnecessary rambling. The team often comes to a quicker decision by remaining on a task level. Conflict is also reduced even though there may be disagreement on issues or information. The conversation is not always completely task oriented; there are words of greeting, thanks, and some occasional humor. Yet the nonverbal aspects of group interaction are limited.

In this sense the computer creates a "leveling" effect among team members. All members are equal. There is no predisposition based on appearance or manner. For example, one team worked with a woman for almost a year before discovering that she was blind. With a braille keyboard she worked as effectively as any other member of the team.

These distributed groups offer many opportunities for participation and interaction among employees in scattered geographic locations. These groups can become effective and cohesive teams, saving travel costs and increasing the communication competence of individuals and teams.

Issue Analysis Teams, Consumer Groups and Community Action Teams

Participative teams also reflect the growing integration of the organization and the community as the organization becomes increasingly proactive and sensitive to the effect of public opinion and priority issues. Community concerns, legislative issues, and consumer attitudes are important to organizational survival in a hostile and competitive economic environment. To remain competitive, the organization must gather increased amounts of information outside the organizational system.

The surrounding community is often the best place to begin collecting information. Most research shows that the public believes that organizations within the community should be concerned with that community's values and problems. Some organizations have community action teams that work directly with local leaders on issues that influence everyone in the community, such as education, unemployment, and crime. These action teams are comprised of local employees and management who deal directly with the community in their day-to-day jobs. They interview opinion leaders in the community and alert the organization to area concerns and issues. This helps the organization to identify with community and local needs in order to create credibility, mutual understanding, and cooperation.

Consumers are also seeking some influence or voice within the organization.

In the future, the customer will be more involved in organization decision making and planning. Focus groups are often used to gather information on customer attitudes, values, and buying preferences. Panels of representative publics are also asked to evaluate products or services in marketing research. Organizations recognize the valuable information that customers or potential customers can provide. Participative teams can help to gather this critical marketing information.

A leading discount pharmacy in Canada established a decentralized personnel management program that includes *progress groups*. Each of these progress groups has five members, one from each department. Their goals are to improve customer service, store operations, and work environment. The five members work with a leader who is often the store manager. Many of their projects are in the area of customer service, and customers are often actively involved in the process. For example, customers are invited to coffee meetings once a month to assess the service being provided by the store. This organization is quite successful in coordinating employees, managers, and customers in an integrated effort at improved quality, productivity and service.[23]

All these factors point to increased participation by consumers and community members in organizational development and decision making. Focus groups and community teams may become more directive, problem-solving groups as the organization makes a stronger link to the community and to the consumers. These integrated teams may be trained in problem-solving techniques and group dynamics to better contribute to organizational development and improved products and services. Cooperative understanding in problem-solving sessions can prevent direct confrontation and protests.

Community members and employees themselves will also be more involved in strategic planning and issue analysis in relation to the organization. Issue analysis teams involve key organizational and community members in discussion and strategic planning. Employee ownership and profit sharing bring employees to the board of directors and other high level strategic planning sessions. These groups analyze issues, predict trends, and plan for a proactive approach to organizational development. However, team members must be responsible and informed if they are to participate.

Participative teams are useful in organizational marketing efforts and in developing organizational ethics, social responsibility, and a sense of accountability to the employees, the community, and the consumers. The objective in this process is information gathering. As information and input become more critical, the organization may have to put additional resources and funds into obtaining this valuable resource. In return for information, the organization may be asked to make a commitment to necessary action and continuing evaluation and development.

Conclusion

The expectations for participation are great and in some cases unrealistically high in bureaucratic, hierarchical organizations. Yet there is much to be said for the future of the participative process. Participation supports many of the trends and predictions for the future of organizations and work patterns. What Kanter terms "idea power" is an essential element in this process of change and innovation, and the "power tools" are information, resources, and support.[8] These tools can help employees to be more productive and innovative within the organization and in the community. Participation creates energy and commitment to individual and organizational development in a changing workplace.

There is no one clear formula or prescription for the participation process. A recent article about "quality gurus" points to the diversity of methods and open disagreement among the nation's top quality and productivity experts. "The gurus seem to agree on certain basic points. . . . But beyond these basics, it is every guru for himself." The author reviews the philosophy and approach of many of the best known people in quality and states that "the whole field is suffused with a fog of jargons, slogans, and statistics."[18]

In spite of elaborate theories and complex formulas, participation is a simple concept based on information sharing, collective decision making, and mutual trust. Participation is not a new concept or a startling breakthrough; it has been practiced for many years in one form or another. Maybe it began with the farm family sitting around the kitchen table to make some decisions about planting. Perhaps it was the supervisor and the two employees who stood puzzling over a machine that just didn't seem to work right. Collective knowledge and resources bring a better decision—one that is more realistic with fewer errors in logic and design, and one that has greater support for implementation.

Each organization must consider participation and employee involvement in terms of its own goals, values, and culture. Yet participation is more than this. Participation is collective idea power produced by employees taking responsibility for quality and productivity, managing their work, and developing their skills and knowledge about the organization and about themselves. Participation is good management.

References

1. Adler, Mortimer J. *A Vision of the Future: Twelve Ideas for a Better Life and a Better Society.* Macmillan, 1984.

2. Diebold, John. *Making the Future Work: Unleashing Our Powers of Innovation for the Decades Ahead.* New York: Simon and Schuster, 1984.

3. Drucker, Peter F. *Managing in Turbulent Times.* New York: Harper & Row, 1980.

4. Field, Lloyd M. "The Practice of Excellence." *Canadian Manager,* 10(2): 6–9. Summer 1985.

5. Gardner, Meryl P. "Creating a Corporate Culture for the Eighties." *Business Horizons,* 28(1): 59–63. Jan./Feb. 1985.

6. Harris, Philip R. *New World, New Ways, New Management: Metaindustrial Organizations.* New York: AMACOM American Management Association, 1983.

7. Kanter, Rosabeth Moss. "The New Workforce Meets the Changing Workplace: Strains,

Dilemmas, and Contradictions in Attempts to Implement Participative and Entrepreneurial Management" *Human Resource Management.* 25(4): 515–537, 1986.

8. _____. *The Change Masters: Innovation for Productivity in the American Corporation.* New York: Simon and Schuster, 1983.

9. Keiser, Thomas C. "The Rules of the Game Have Changed." *Training,* 23(1): 43–47. Jan. 1986.

10. Kerr, Steven, Kenneth Hill, and Laurie Broedling. "The First-Line Supervisor: Phasing Out or Here to Stay?" *Academy of Management Review,* 26(2): 33–44. Jan. 1986.

11. Lawler, Edward E. III and Gerald E. Ledford Jr. "Skill-Based Pay: A Concept That's Catching On." *Management Review.* 76(2): 46–51. Feb. 1987.

12. Lawler, Edward E. III, and Susan A. Mohrman. "Quality Circles After the Fad," *Harvard Business Review,* 63(1): 64–75. Jan./Feb. 1985.

13. Leach, John J., and B. J. Chakiris. "The Dwindling Future of Work in America." *Training and Development Journal,* April 1985.

14. Leana, Carrie R. "Power Relinquishment Versus Power Sharing: Theoretical Clarification and Empirical Comparison of Delegation and Participation." *Journal of Applied Psychology,* 72(2): 228–233. May 1987.

15. Lippitt, Gordon. *Organizational Renewal.* Englewood Cliffs, NJ: Prentice-Hall, 1969.

16. London, Manuel. "Employee-Guided Management: Steps for Involving Employees in Decisions and Actions." *Leadership and Organizational Development Journal,* UK, 30(8): 3–8. 1985.

17. Long, Richard J. and Malcolm Warner. "Organizations, Participation and Recession: An Analysis of Recent Evidence." *Industrial Relations,* 42(1): 65–88. Winter, 1987.

18. Main, Jeremy. "Under the Spell of the Quality Gurus." *Fortune,* 18 August 1986: 30–34.

19. McGaughey, William Jr. *A Shorter Workweek in the 1980's.* White Bear Lake, MN: Thistlerose Publications, 1981.

20. Miller, Lawrence M. "Creating the New High Commitment Culture." *Supervisory Management,* 30(8): 2–28. Aug. 1985.

21. Mink, Oscar G., James M. Shultz, and Barbara P. Mink. *Developing and Managing Open Organizations: A Model of Methods for Maximizing Organizational Potential.* Austin, TX: Learning Concepts, 1979.

22. Naisbitt, John. *Megatrends: The New Directions Transforming Our Lives.* New York: Warner Books, 1982.

23. Poulin, Fernande. "People Involvement in a Multi-Outlet Retail Organization: A Case Study." Paper presented at the International Association of Quality Circles Conference, Baltimore, MD, 1986.

24. Richardson, Peter R. "Courting Greater Employee Involvement Through Participative Management." *Sloan Management Review,* 16(2): 33–44. Winter 1985.

25. Yankelovich, Daniel. *New Rules: Searching for Self-Fulfillment in a World Turned Upside Down.* New York: Random House, 1981.

INDEX